DEPARTMENT OF THE NAVY
HEADQUARTERS UNITED STATES MARINE CORPS
3000 MARINE CORPS PENTAGON
WASHINGTON, DC 20350-3000

I0500420

MARINE CORPS READINESS REPORTING STANDARD OPERATING PROCEDURES (SOP)

DEPARTMENT OF THE NAVY
HEADQUARTERS UNITED STATES MARINE CORPS
3000 MARINE CORPS PENTAGON
WASHINGTON, DC 20350-3000

MCO 3000.13
POR
30 Jul 2010

MARINE CORPS ORDER 3000.13

From: Commandant of the Marine Corps
To: Distribution List

Subj: MARINE CORPS READINESS REPORTING STANDARD OPERATING
      PROCEDURES (SOP)

Ref: (a) CJCSI 3401.02A, "Global Status of Resources and
         Training System (GSORTS)," June 12, 2008
     (b) CJCSM 3150.02A, "Global Status of Resources and
         Training System (GSORTS)," April 29, 2004 (NOTAL)
     (c) DOD Directive 7730.65, "Department of Defense
         Readiness Reporting System (DRRS)," April 23, 2007
     (d) MCO 5311.1D
     (e) MCO 3400.3F
     (f) MCO 3000.11D
     (g) MCO 1553.3A
     (h) MCO 3500.26A
     (i) MCO 3125.1B
     (j) MCO 3500.14
     (k) NAVMC 3500.14B
     (l) NAVMC 3500.18A
     (m) NAVMC 3500.70
     (n) SECNAV M-5210.1

Encl: (1) Marine Corps Readiness Reporting SOP Guidance

Reports Required: I. Defense Readiness Reporting System-
                        Marine Corps (Report Control Symbol
                        EXEMPT), par. 4.a.(2)

1. Situation. To promulgate policies and procedures for
reporting readiness on Marine Corps organizations. This Order
amplifies the policies, procedures and reporting requirements
delineated in references (a) through (d).

2. Cancellation. MCO P3000.13D and Interim Defense Readiness
Reporting System (DRRS) Policy & Procedures for Marine Corps
Units and Installations.

DISTRIBUTION STATEMENT A: Approved for public release;
distribution is unlimited.

3. Mission. This Order provides policy and procedures for reporting readiness for units, selected installations, and other organizations in the Marine Corps per references (a) through (n). Procedural "how to" guidance is contained in the appendices.

4. Execution

   a. Commander's Intent and Concept of Operations

      (1) Commander's Intent. The Marine Corps will meet its Title 10 Readiness reporting responsibilities by providing both capability and resource related assessments to meet Service and Department of Defense (DOD) requirements.

      (2) Concept of Operations. The Marine Corps will maintain a single, uniform system for the preparation, approval, and maintenance of a readiness reporting system. This reporting requirement is exempt from reports control per reference (n), part IV, paragraph 7.h. Future enhancements to the Defense Readiness Reporting System Marine Corps (DRRS-MC) in support of evolving DOD requirements will be captured in subsequent changes to this Order.

   b. Subordinate Element Missions

      (1) Deputy Commandant for Plans, Policy and Operations (DC PP&O)

         (a) Establish Service policy, procedures, training, and guidance on unit readiness reporting.

         (b) In coordination with DC I&L, establish Service policy, procedures, and guidance on installation readiness reporting in DRRS-MC.

         (c) Maintain DRRS-MC per applicable Joint and DoD directives.

         (d) Coordinate proposed Service policies and procedures with other Services, Combatant Commands, the Joint Staff, Defense Information Systems Agency (DISA), Deputy Under Secretary of Defense (Readiness), and the Office of the Secretary of Defense.

(e) Develop and review every four years mission statements and core mission essential task lists (METLs) for ground combat element organizations that DC PP&O is assigned Marine Air Ground Task Force (MAGTF) advocacy. Develop and review standards used for MET assessment. Provide METs and standards to DC, CD&I and COMMMARFORCOM.

(f) Register units, organizations, and installations in DRRS-MC. Coordinate with DC I&L on which installations will be designated to report in DRRS-MC.

(g) Integrate USMC readiness initiatives and serve as the functional advocate for DRRS-MC.

(h) Coordinate the activation, deactivation, and reassignment of Marine Corps units with the Deputy Commandant, Combat Development & Integration (CD&I), Total Force Structure Division (TFSD).

(i) Post and maintain an updated DRRS-MC User's Guide on PP&O's portal for force and supporting establishment commanders.

(2) Deputy Commandant, Installations and Logistics (DC, I&L)

(a) In coordination with DC PP&O, establish Service policy, procedures, and guidance on installation readiness reporting in DRRS-MC.

(b) Coordinate proposed Service installation reporting policies and procedures with other Services, Combatant Commands, the Joint Staff, Defense Information Systems Agency (DISA), and the Office of the Secretary of Defense.

(c) Coordinate the designation and registration of selected installations to report in DRRS-MC with DC PP&O and DC CD&I.

(d) Integrate USMC readiness initiatives relative to installations.

(e) Develop and review every four years mission statements and core mission essential task lists (METLs) for logistic combat element organizations and installations that DC I&L is assigned MAGTF advocacy. Develop and review standards used for MET assessment. Provide METs and standards to DC, CD&I and COMMMARFORCOM.

(f) Identify the readiness reportable ground principal end items (PEI) and mission essential equipment (MEE) selected for readiness reporting.

(3) <u>Deputy Commandant, Aviation</u>

(a) Coordinate with PP&O on policy, procedures, and guidance for aviation unit readiness reporting.

(b) Develop and review every four years mission statements and core mission essential task lists (METLs) for aviation combat element organizations that DC Aviation is assigned MAGTF advocacy. Develop and review standards used for MET assessment. Provide METs and standards to DC, CD&I and COMMMARFORCOM.

(4) <u>Deputy Commandant, Combat Development & Integration (CD&I)</u>

(a) Manage, coordinate, maintain, and serve as the primary review authority of the Marine Corps Task List (MCTL) and update it as required. Provide periodic examination of the MCTL to reflect installation METLs, Unit Core METLs, Named Operation METLs, and Concept Plan/Operation Plan (CONPLAN/OPLAN) METLs. Define doctrinal tasks and support operational reporting requirements.

(b) Coordinate the activation, deactivation, and reassignment of Marine Corps units and installations with PP&O and I&L.

(c) Develop and review every four years mission statements and core mission essential task lists (METLs) for command element organizations that DC CD&I is assigned MAGTF advocacy. Develop and review standards used for MET assessment.

(d) Assist Deputy Commandants, Advocates and the Marine Corps Component Commanders (MARFORs) in the development of Common Core METLs with conditions and standards for all like-type units and installations.

(e) Establish and maintain a Service organizational database for unit METs and associated standards.

(f) Incorporate standardized Unit Core METLs and associated training standards in Ground and Aviation T&R Manuals.

(g) Identify, develop, fund and administer an online distance learning (DL) DRRS-MC training course. Obtain input from PP&O (POR), Advocates, the MARFORs, and Commanders of designated Marine Corps installations regarding DL course requirements.

(5) <u>Commanding General, Marine Corps Forces Command (MARFORCOM)</u>

(a) Support the development and periodic review of common Core METs and associated standards for all like-type conventional units.

(b) Coordinate with DC CD&I to load Core METs and associated standards for like-type conventional units into the Service organizational MET database.

(c) Develop templates for unit Named Operations and OPLAN/CONPLAN METLs.

(d) Integrate Named Operation and OPLAN/CONPLAN METL development into force sourcing actions.

(6) <u>Marine Corps Component Commanders (MARFORCOM, MARFORPAC, MARFORSOC, MARFORCENT, MARFOREUR, MARFORSOUTH, MARFORSTRAT, MARFORNORTH, MARFORAF, MARFORCYBERCOM, MARFORKOREA, MARFORRES)</u>

(a) Inform the supporting MARFOR (MARFORCOM, MARFORPAC, MARFORRES, MARFORSOC) when OPLAN/CONPLAN assessment requires assigned units to develop and report against OPLAN/CONPLAN METLs. MARFORSOC is the exception, when they provide forces to Theater Special Operations Commands (TSOCs).

(b) Establish procedures to monitor the readiness reporting of subordinate units for accuracy, timeliness, and validity. Direct corrective action as required.

(c) Support subordinate units' development of Named Operation and OPLAN/CONPLAN METLs. Inform HQMC (PP&O), MCCDC, and MARFORCOM if such METLs need to become the focus of resourcing and training efforts instead of Core Unit METLs.

(d) Integrate Named Operation and OPLAN/CONPLAN METLs into unit deployment orders as appropriate.

(e) Support DRRS-MC development, testing and training.

(7) <u>Marine Corps Forces Special Operations Command (MARFORSOC)</u>

(a) Support the development and periodic review of common Core METs and associated standards for special operations units.

(b) Coordinate with CD&I to load common Core METs and associated standards for all like-type special operations units into the Service organizational MET database.

(c) Develop templates for special operations unit Named Operation and OPLAN/CONPLAN METLs.

(d) Support DRRS-MC development, testing, and training.

(8) <u>U.S. Marine Corps Bases Atlantic and Pacific</u>

(a) Supervise DRRS-MC reporting for selected installations upon direction of HQMC, I&L.

(b) Coordinate DRRS-MC development, testing, and training for subordinate installations.

(9) <u>Reporting Units, Organizations, and Installations.</u> Assess their organizations in DRRS-MC.

5. <u>Administration and Logistics</u>

a. Recommendations concerning the contents of this Order may be forwarded to CMC PP&O (POR) via the appropriate chain-of-command.

b. Records created as a result of this directive shall include records management requirements to ensure the proper maintenance and use of records, regardless of format or medium, to promote accessibility and authorized retention per the approved records schedule and reference (n).

6. Command and Signal

a. Command. This Order is applicable to the Marine Corps Total Force.

b. Signal. This Order is effective the date signed.

T. D. WALDHAUSER
Deputy Commandant for
Plans, Policies and Operations

DISTRIBUTION: PCN 10203045300

Copy to: 8145001 USCINCSTRATACOM/J3 (10)
Joint Staff USCINCCENT/ccj3 (10)
J-1 USCINCEUCOM/ECJ3-FD (10)
J-38 USCINCTRANSCOM/DOCR (10)
J-6I USCINCPACCOM/J34 (10)
J-7/EAD/JDED USCINCSOUTHCOM/SCJ3-OPOS-JOC (10)
DISA/JSSC (1) USCINCSPACECOM/J-3CO (10)
CSA/DAMO-ODR (5) USCINCSOCOM/J3 (10)
CSAF/XOOOC (5) USJTFORCESCMD/J331 (10)
CNO/OP642E (5)

LOCATOR SHEET

Subj: MARINE CORPS READINESS REPORTING STANDING OPERATING
       PROCEDURES (SHORT TITLE: MARINE CORPS READINESS SOP)

LOCATION: _____
                (Indicates the location(s) of copy(ies) of this Order.)

RECORD OF CHANGES

Log completed change action as indicated.

Change Number	Date of Change	Date Entered	Signature of Person Incorporated Change

TABLE OF CONTENTS

Chapter 4   **MET ASSESSMENTS**

Chapter 5   **TRAINING**

Chapter 6   **CHEMICAL, BIOLOGICAL, AND NUCLEAR (CBRN) DEFENSE**

Chapter 1

Readiness Overview

1. <u>Purpose</u>. This Chapter outlines general policy for operational readiness reporting. It includes information on which organizations report, reporting occasions, reporting channels, security, and the release of readiness data outside of the Marine Corps.

2. <u>Policy</u>. Reference (a) contains the general provisions, detailed instructions, and formats to submit readiness data in support of joint requirements. Supplemental instructions are provided by this Order. This Order is the governing authority for all Marine Corps readiness reporting requirements. Development or use of any additional software, reporting formats, local standards or definitions within any part of readiness reporting requires prior authorization from DC PP&O (POR).

3. <u>Background</u>

a. <u>Readiness</u>. Readiness is defined as the ability of U.S. military forces to fight and meet the demands of the national military strategy. Readiness is the synthesis of two distinct but interrelated levels.

(1) <u>Unit Readiness</u>. The ability to provide capabilities required by the combatant commanders to execute their assigned missions. This is derived from the ability of each unit to deliver the outputs for which it was designed. Unit readiness is reported by the military services.

(2) <u>Joint Readiness</u>. This is the combatant commander's (CCDR's) or Joint Task Force (JTF) Commander's ability to integrate and synchronize ready combat and support forces to execute assigned missions. Accurate and timely unit readiness reports are essential for Joint Readiness reporting.

b. <u>Legal Requirement To Report Readiness</u>. Title 10, section 153a.3.C., United States Code (USC) directs the Chairman of the Joint Chiefs of Staff to advise the Secretary of Defense on critical deficiencies and strengths in force capabilities identified during the preparation and review of contingency plans. Title 10, section 117, USC directed the Secretary of Defense to establish a comprehensive readiness reporting system that would measure in an objective, accurate, and timely manner the capability of the U.S. military to carry out the National Security Strategy, Defense Planning Guidance, and the National Military Strategy. Title 10, section 5042b.2, U.S.C. directs Headquarters, Marine Corps, to investigate and report upon their efficiency and preparation to support military operations by combatant commanders.

c. <u>Uses</u>. Readiness information supports in priority order: crisis response planning, deliberate or peacetime planning, and management responsibilities to organize, train, and equip combat-ready forces for the unified commands. Readiness reporting information is also used in: Service testimony, reports to Congress, the Chairman of the Joint Chief of Staff's Readiness System and other venues.

4. <u>Scope</u>. This Order applies to all Marine Corps readiness reporting organizations.

5. <u>Reporting Organizations</u>

a. <u>Organizations Required to Report</u>. Combat, combat support, and combat service support units of the Marine Air Ground Task Forces (MAGTFs), MARFORs, and designated organizations and installations will report their readiness. Each type of organization is deployable, designed for warfighting, or provides support to the warfighting Marine. These will include designated task organized units.

b. <u>Organizations Not Under MARFOR Operational Control</u>. Marine Corps organizations passed OPCON to a non-Marine Corps command will submit their reports through DRRS-MC. This applies to units in contingency operations and aviation squadrons participating in Navy carrier integration.

c. <u>Non-Marine Corps Organizations OPCON to Marine Organizations</u>. Those organizations will report their readiness per their channels, not in DRRS-MC. Exceptions may be requested of PP&O, POR, through the chain of command.

d. <u>Readiness Reporting Organizations</u>. Only organizations designated by PP&O, POR will submit readiness reports. Requests for organizations to report in DRRS-MC will be forwarded to PP&O, POR through the chain of command.

6. <u>Core and Assigned Readiness Assessments</u>. The readiness reporting system allows commanders of reporting organizations to uniformly determine and accurately report their organizations'

ability to accomplish the core (wartime) mission for which the organization was designed via a C-level and core mission capability assessment. When applicable, commanders will also capture their organizations' ability to accomplish assigned missions via the Percent Effective (PCTEF) level and an assigned mission capability assessment. All these assessments can be captured in a single report.

a. C-Level and PCTEF Assessments. Both assessments indicate the degree to which a unit has achieved prescribed levels of fill for personnel and equipment, the materiel condition of available equipment, and the training proficiency status of the unit. C-level and PCTEF are discussed in Chapter 7.

b. Core and Assigned Mission Capability Assessments. The most significant aspect of readiness reporting is the requirement for Commanders to assess their organizations' capabilities to accomplish their mission essential tasks (METs) to specified conditions and standards. Those assessments are then used by Commanders to assess their organizations' capabilities to accomplish their missions. These assessments are discussed in Chapter 4.

7. Reporting Occasions. Reports will be submitted within 24 hours of the occasions listed in Table 1-1 for the organizations specified. Units will continue to report when deployed for training, deployed in response to a crisis, deployed in execution of an OPLAN, and in combat. Occasions that require the report to include PCTEF/assigned mission capability assessments are shown in the right most column of Table 1-1.

Table 1-1.--Reporting Occasions

Occasion	Units	MARFOR	Installations	PCTEF/ Assign Msn
30 days since last report	X	X		
90 days since last report			X	
Activation or deactivation	X	X	X	
Change in C-Level	X			
Change in Percent Effective (PCTEF)	X			X

Change in core Mission Assessment (Yes, Qualified Yes, No)	X	X	X	
Change in assigned Mission Assessment (Yes, Qualified Yes, No)	X	X	X	X
Change in Administrative Control (ADCON) or Operational Control (OPCON)	X		X	
Change of location of command element	X		X	
Change of geographic location of unit's personnel or equipment (e.g. mobilized reserve unit's arrival at Site of Initial Activation, a unit's arrival at CAX, or arrival overseas)	X			
Employed in support of an in-lieu mission (one that does not match the core mission)	X	X	X	X
Assignment to Named Operations (e.g. Operation Iraqi Freedom) or Operational Plan/Concept Plan (OPLAN/CONPLAN) by D-90	X	X	X	X
Assignment to Security, Transition, and Reconstruction (SSTR) mission	X			X

Receipt of an order to execute any of these missions: homeland defense, homeland security, peacekeeping, peace enforcement, humanitarian assistance, consequence management, counter-drug, civil disturbance, and natural disaster relief (including wildfire fighting)	X	X	X	X
Receipt of an alert, formal warning, or execute order for deployment or NLT 90 days prior to deployment, whichever comes first	X			X
12 months prior to a Reserve unit's planned activation date	X			X
Mobilization of Reserve unit	X			

a. Increased Reporting Frequency. The Chairman of the Joint Chiefs of Staff may require organizations to report more frequently. Combatant commanders may require assigned units, or units over whom they exercise OPCON, to report more frequently. DC PP&O, and Marine Forces (MARFORs) may also require increased reporting frequency and more detailed remarks to provide updated information for crisis planning.

b. Reporting Intervals. MARFORs may set submission dates, within the reporting occasions, to stagger the reporting intervals for organizations OPCON to them (e.g. battalions report on 1st of month, regiments report on 10th of month).

8. Reporting Channels. Readiness reports are the responsibility of the organization commander and must reflect the commander's best military judgment regarding the organization's readiness. Organizations submit their reports

directly into DRRS-MC, and the use of DRRS-MC software is mandatory. Coordination of readiness issues with higher, supported, and supporting commands ensures a shared understanding of unit capabilities and any support that may be required. Commanders and staffs must avoid actions which may impair the submission of timely, accurate, and complete readiness assessments by subordinate organizations. Higher headquarters will not require higher level review of reports prior to submission or direct minimum levels of reported readiness.

a. Edit of Reports. Report originators will be notified of reports processed and errors detected. Erroneous reports will be corrected and resubmitted within 24 hours of notification.

b. Review of DRRS-MC Data. DRRS-MC resource data is maintained in the GSORTS database by the Defense Information Systems Agency. Resource data and mission and MET assessments can be accessed through DRRS-MC with the Marine Readiness Management Output Tool (MRMOT). Reporting organizations at all levels must develop an audit program to periodically check readiness reports for accuracy. Higher headquarters are not authorized to change subordinate organization readiness reports, except to correct computation errors or administrative errors.

9. Security Classification

a. The classification of readiness data will be based on the highest classified item in the report. Top Secret information will not be reported. Protection of classified information shall be per: DOD Instruction 5200.01 (DOD Information Security Program and Protection of Sensitive Compartmented Information; SECNAVINST 5510.36A), Department Of The Navy (DON) Information Security Program (ISP) Instruction; and the Chairman of Joint Chiefs of Staff Manual on GSORTS (CJCSM 3150.02A).

b. The policy guidance contained in this paragraph is specifically applicable to reports that are submitted in compliance with the provisions of this Order and to information contained in or extracted from those reports following their submission. The provisions of this paragraph are not applicable to information regarding personnel status, equipment status, or training status of organizations, people or equipment that resides in or is derived from other databases or systems.

c. <u>Confidential</u>. C-level, PCTEF, and core/assigned capability mission assessments for a battalion, squadron, installation or smaller unit are confidential.

d. <u>Secret</u>. C-level, PCTEF, and core/assigned capability mission assessments for organizations larger than a battalion, squadron, or installation are secret.

e. <u>Top Secret</u>. Top secret information will not be included in readiness reports.

10. <u>Release and Access to Reports</u>. Marine Corps readiness information will not be released outside the Department of Defense without the written approval of PP&O, POR. Outside agencies with a valid need-to-know and the appropriate clearance should submit requests to PP&O, POR.

11. <u>Codes for Report Submissions</u>. Appendix G contains codes for readiness report submissions that are not contained in the other chapters and appendices.

Chapter 2

Personnel

1. <u>Purpose</u>. This chapter outlines policy for personnel reporting.

2. <u>Policy</u>. Reporting of personnel to determine a Personnel-rating (P-rating) is based on the unit's ability to provide deployable, military occupational specialty (MOS) qualified personnel to accomplish its missions. It is one of the four measured areas that are factors in determining a unit's C-level. P-ratings may also be used as part of the standards for a unit's METs. Reportable personnel will be accounted for by only one organization at a time.

3. <u>Scope</u>. This section applies to Marine Corps readiness reporting units, not installations or MARFORs. Intermediate level commands will provide a subjective assessment of their personnel resource rating based upon the resource ratings of subordinate units.

4. <u>Reporting Requirements</u>. Personnel readiness policy is explained in this chapter. Personnel guidance on reporting procedures, mandatory remarks, and reason codes are contained in Appendix A.

   a. <u>P-Rating</u>. Units will determine the P-rating based on the lower percentage of the PERSONNEL STRENGTH and MOS FILL calculations. Figure 2-1 depicts the formulas for calculating these percentages. Task organized units and units detaching personnel to task organized units will comply with paragraph 5 of this chapter when calculating personnel percentages. Table 2-1 depicts how the percentages determine the P-rating. The P-rating will be calculated as of the time of the report and will not be a future projection. P-ratings of less than 1 require reason codes and remarks per Appendix A.

Figure 2-1.--Personnel Percentages

Personnel Strength Percentage
= (Assigned Strength – Nondeployables/Structure Strength) X 100
MOS Fill Percentage
= (MOS Fill – Nondeployables/Structure Strength) X 100

Table 2-1.--P Ratings

Rule	P1	P2	P3	P4
Personnel Strength	≥90%	80-89%	70-79%	<70%
MOS Fill	≥85%	75-84%	65-74%	<65%

b. <u>Structure Strength</u>. The Total Force Structure Management System (TFSMS) is the authoritative source for obtaining a unit's table of organization (T/O) Structure Strength data; minus any individual mobilization augmentation (IMA) billets or unfilled Navy billets identified with a "M" code (medical billets to be augmented by the hospital staff). Site support personnel will not be counted in Reserve units. Task organized units will obtain their personnel Structure Strength from the unit's manning documents. Task organized units and the units providing personnel to task organized units will adjust their Structure Strength per paragraph 5 of this chapter. Occasionally, the majority of a unit will deploy, but still retain personnel at their home station. Those units will compute their structure strength per paragraph 6 of this chapter.

c. <u>Assigned Strength</u>. The Marine Corps Total Force Structure System (MCTFS) is the authoritative source for unit personnel status, which should be used to help determine the Assigned Strength. Reporting units will list their entire assigned strength, minus any contingency billets (read as a "C" type billet on a unit's T/O) or unfilled Navy billets identified with an "M" code (medical billets to be augmented by the hospital staff). Task organized units and the units providing personnel to task organized units will adjust their Assigned Strength per paragraph 5 of this chapter. Units that are deployed, but still retain personnel at home station will compute their assigned strength per paragraph 6 of this chapter.

d. <u>MOS Fill</u>. The MOS FILL is determined by taking the number of personnel matched against T/O line number billets by MOS. A unit will report Marines filling T/O billets using either a primary or additional MOS, but not both. One Marine cannot fill two billet lines, even if that Marine has two MOSs. Each person will be aligned with a specific T/O line number by MOS, and the rank may vary one above or one below that listed in the T/O, if it's the same MOS. Marines assigned to billets such as Scout Sniper, will use their primary MOS with a necessary skill designator to match against the unit's T/O (i.e., 0369 with a billet MOS of 8541 Scout Sniper). In cases where line numbers require more than one MOS, each MOS must match to count as an MOS match.

    e. <u>Non-Deployable Personnel</u>. The criteria for determining a non-deployable status and the codes for listing them are depicted in Tables G-4 and G-5.

    f. <u>Critical MOSs</u>. Units will identify the three most critical PMOSs that have the largest detrimental impact on the unit's readiness per Appendix A.

5. <u>Task-Organization</u>. Task organized units gaining personnel and the units providing them personnel will adjust their personnel quantities. Coordination must occur between the task organized and providing units to avoid double counting of personnel. Remarks explaining the personnel adjustments will remain in the task organized and providing units' reports until the detachments are returned to the providing units or transferred elsewhere.

    a. <u>Task Organized Units Gaining Personnel</u>. Task organized units that receive detachments of personnel will increase their Assigned Strength, Structure Strength, and MOS Fill quantities.

    b. <u>Units Providing Personnel to Task Organized Units</u>. The Assigned Strength and MOS Fill quantities will be subtracted from the providing unit(s). Do not subtract the Structure Strength from the providing unit.

6. <u>Personnel Remaining Behind From Deployment</u>. When an active duty unit deploys and has personnel that still belong to the unit remaining behind, the commander will still consider them in the P-rating calculation and C-level assessment. They will not be considered in PCTEF, assigned MET and mission assessments. If some of these personnel are subsequently transferred to another unit, their quantity is removed from the assigned strength, not the structure strength. This policy is not applicable to Reserve units, because remain behind personnel are transferred to another unit upon deployment.

7. <u>Employ/Deploy Codes</u>. When five percent (5%) or more of a unit's personnel are detached to deploy with another unit, the

providing unit will use the employ/deployed codes from
Appendix G, Table G-6 to report the percentage deployed.

Enclosure (1)

Chapter 3

Equipment

1. <u>Purpose</u>. This chapter outlines policy for equipment reporting for both equipment and supplies on hand (S-rating), and equipment condition (R-rating). The S-rating is a materiel measurement of an organization's possessed equipment quantity against its designed requirement. The R-rating indicates the materiel condition of the organization's possessed equipment.

2. <u>Policy</u>. Reporting on equipment to determine a S-rating and a R-rating is based on the unit's ability to provide the quantities and quality of equipment to accomplish its missions. The S and R ratings are two of the four measured areas that are factors in determining a unit's C-level. S and R-ratings may also be used as part of the conditions for an organization's METs. Equipment will be accounted for by only one organization at a time, and the present materiel status, not future projections, will be used. Active and Reserve units will compute their S and R-ratings in the same way.

3. <u>Scope</u>. This section applies to Marine Corps readiness reporting units. It does not apply to installations or MARFORs. Intermediate level commands will provide a subjective assessment of their equipment ratings based upon their subordinate units' S and R ratings.

4. <u>Reporting Requirements</u>. Materiel readiness policy is explained in this chapter. Materiel guidance on reporting procedures, mandatory remarks, and reason codes are contained in Appendix B.

5. <u>Reportable Equipment</u>. Selected pieces of equipment are designated to accurately capture the equipment readiness of Marine Corps units. The selected equipment is reported as either mission essential equipment (MEE) or principal end items (PEI).

   a. <u>Ground Equipment</u>. Reference (f) defines MEE and PEI for ground equipment and sets forth the procedures for updating them. Updated MEE and PEI are published in Marine Corps Bulletin 3000.

   b. <u>Aircraft and Aviation Support Equipment</u>. Flying squadrons, to include MEU(ACE) designated squadrons, will consider their aircraft as MEE when calculating their S and R-ratings. Flying squadrons will not calculate aviation support equipment as PEI. MALS will calculate S and R-ratings using aviation support equipment as PEI.

6. <u>S-Rating: Equipment and Supplies</u>. Units will calculate a S-rating as of the time of the report and report the lowest S-rating between the MEE and PEI calculations. Task organized units and units detaching equipment to task organized units will comply with paragraph 8 of this chapter when calculating S-ratings. Table 3-1 depicts the criteria for these calculations.

Table 3-1.--Equipment and Supplies (S-Rating)

Rule	S1	S2	S3	S4
1. <u>Mission Essential Equipment (MEE)</u> Total Service-selected mission-essential equipment possessed divided by prescribed wartime requirements [UTR]	≥90%	80-89%	65-79%	<65%
Total In Reporting Status aircraft possessed divided by prescribed wartime requirement (PMAA)	≥90%	80-89%	60-79%	<60%
2. <u>Support Equipment (PEI)</u> Total Service-selected principal end-items possessed divided by prescribed wartime requirement [UTR]	≥90%	80-89%	65-79%	<65%

    a. <u>Prescribed Wartime Requirement</u>. The Total Force Structure Management System (TFSMS) is the authoritative source for obtaining a unit's table of equipment (T/E) data for ground equipment. The T/E prescribed wartime requirement appears in the AAO column, which will be changed in the future to read Unit T/E Requirement (UTR). The Primary Mission Authorized Aircraft (PMAA) quantity is the prescribed wartime requirement for tactical aircraft. The PMAA is published in the Marine Aviation Plan. Task organized units will use their sourcing document or equipment density list (EDL) for their prescribed wartime requirement. The prescribed wartime requirement for aviation support equipment comes from the Support Equipment Resources Management Information System (SERMIS).

b. <u>Possessed Equipment</u>. Ground and aviation supply regulations determine the possession status of equipment. Excess possessed equipment (quantities above the prescribed PEI and MEE wartime requirement) will not be used to calculate the S or R-ratings for non-intermediate units, but will be mentioned in the report's remarks.

c. <u>Intermediate Level Commands</u>. Intermediate commands should consider the impact of any excess equipment in their subordinate units when making a subjective S-rating assessment.

7. <u>R-Rating: Equipment Condition</u>. Units will calculate a R-rating as of the time of the report and report the lowest R-rating between the MEE and PEI calculations. Applicable maintenance directives determine a mission capable status. Excess possessed equipment (quantities above the prescribed wartime requirement) will not be used in the R-rating. Further guidance on aircraft status is defined in OPNAVINST 5442.4 and OPNAVINST 4790.2. Table 3-2 depicts the criteria for the R-rating calculations.

Table 3-2.—-Equipment Condition (R-Rating)

Rule	R1	R2	R3	R4
1. <u>Mission Essential Equipment (MEE)</u> Total Service-selected mission-essential equipment available and "mission capable" divided by total possessed	≥90%	70-89%	60-69%	<60%
Total In Reporting Status aircraft mission capable divided by total aircraft In Reporting Status	≥75%	60-74%	50-59%	<50%

2. Principal End Item (PEI) Total Service-selected principal end-items available and mission capable divided by the total possessed	≥90%	70-89%	60-69%	<60%

8. **Task Organization**. Task organized units and the units providing them equipment will adjust their equipment quantities as described below. Coordination must occur between the task organized and providing units to avoid double counting of equipment. The adjustments will remain in the task organized and providing units' reports until the detachments are returned to the providing units or transferred elsewhere.

    a. **Task Organized Units Gaining Equipment**. Task organized units that receive detachments of equipment will increase their possessed and prescribed wartime requirement quantities.

    b. **Units Providing Equipment to Task Organized Units**. The possessed quantities will be subtracted from the providing unit(s). Do not subtract the prescribed wartime requirement quantities.

9. **Equipment Remaining Behind From Deployment**. When an active duty unit deploys and has equipment that still belongs to the unit remaining behind, the commander will still include that equipment in the S and R-rating calculations and the C-level assessment. They will not be considered in PCTEF or assigned MET and mission assessments. This policy is not applicable to Reserve units, because remain behind equipment is transferred to another unit when they deploy.

10. **Employ/Deploy Codes**. When five percent (5%) or more of a unit's equipment is detached to deploy with another unit, the providing unit will use the employ/deployed codes from Appendix G, Table G-6 to report the percentage deployed.

Chapter 4

MET Assessments

1. <u>Purpose</u>. This chapter outlines policy for assessing mission essential tasks (METs).

2. <u>Policy</u>. METs will be developed per references (g) and (h). Core METs are published within Training and Readiness manuals and form the foundation for a community's T&R standards. A mission essential task list (METL) contains the list of a command's essential tasks with appropriate conditions and performance standards to assure successful mission accomplishment. The assessment of METs will be based on the organization's present state, not a future projection. Guidance on MET assessment procedures is contained in Appendix C.

3. <u>Scope</u>. All readiness reporting units (including intermediate commands), installations, and MARFORs will assess their METs.

4. <u>MET Assessment</u>

a. <u>General</u>. A MET is an event in which a unit or organization must be proficient to be capable of accomplishing an appropriate portion of its wartime mission. All readiness reporting Marine Corps organizations will have a mission essential task list (METL). Assessments at all levels will include evaluations of the resources available and training readiness to perform METs to prescribed standards. The assessments will assist the commander in determining the organization's ability to execute core and assigned missions. Reference (h) provides a common language that commanders can use to document their warfighting requirements as METs. The METs in reference (h) are architecturally linked to the Universal Joint Task List (UJTL), which includes strategic-national, strategic-theater, and operational level of war tasks used by joint task forces and Combatant Commanders.

b. <u>Types of MET Assessments</u>. Commanders will assess METs for three types of missions: Core, assigned Major Operational Plans/Concept Plans (OPLANs/CONPLANs), and assigned Named Operations.

(1) <u>Core METs</u>. Core METs define the design capabilities of a unit and are developed using tasks documented in the Marine Corps Task List (MCTL), reference (h). Core METs are reflected

in the T&R manuals and provide the foundation for a community's T&R standards. The conditions and standards for training to Core METs are reflected by events which serve as the measures to gauge readiness against the performance of the task. Personnel and equipment standards for Core METs are developed by DC CD&I Total Force Structure and can be found within the Service organizational MET database. Core METs are standardized for all units of the same type and are used to develop the community's T&R Manual. Core METs form the basis for the METL and additional METs are added or refined as required. Units without approved Core METs will establish their own (with conditions and standards), based on established doctrine, METLs of similar units, higher headquarters' METLs, and Marine Corps publications. The MCTL contains Marine Corps tasks approved by Marine Corps Combat Development Command, Combat Development and Integration (MCCDC, CD&I).

(2) <u>Major OPLAN/CONPLAN METs</u>. Major OPLANs/CONPLANs are plans that require level four detail (established Time-Phased Force & Deployment Data (TPFDD)), per the Contingency Planning Guidance. When tasked by higher headquarters, units that have been assigned in support of major OPLANs/CONPLANs will use OPLAN/CONPLAN specific METs and will report their readiness to support these missions. The commander checks the baseline METL derived from core tasks and adjusts to add, delete, and/or modify METs as appropriate during mission assessment of the warplan. The supported Marine Corps Component Commanders are the approving authorities for OPLAN/CONPLAN specific METs for their major subordinate units, and will ensure unit METLs support Combatant Commander capability requirements. U.S. Marine Corps Forces Command will develop and maintain METL templates for various missions (e.g., provisional security operations) to support this process.

(3) <u>Named Operation METs</u>. Named operations are those operations designated as such by the Joint Chiefs of Staff (e.g. Operation IRAQI FREEDOM). They will be assessed when 25 percent or more of a unit deploys or prepares to deploy in support of a named operation. Core METs, OPLAN/CONPLAN METs, METL templates, and deployment guidance provide the basis for the development and refinement of named operation METs. When such an operation or deployment requires specific or additional skills, the commander revises the unit's METL accordingly and submits to the next higher level of command for approval.

5. <u>Assessment Definitions</u>. The Commander will assess his METs as Yes, Qualified Yes, or No. The definitions for those

assessments are below. Table C-1 in Appendix C provides more in-depth information to assist with MET assessment.

    a. <u>Yes "Y" Assessment</u>. The organization can accomplish the task to standard under the specified conditions. A "Y" assessment should reflect demonstrated performance in training or operations whenever possible. A "Y" assessment indicates an organization possesses the necessary resources or those resources explicitly identified in its MET to allow it to execute when ordered.

    b. <u>Qualified Yes "Q" Assessment</u>. The organization is expected to accomplish the task to standard under most conditions, but this performance has not been observed or demonstrated in training or operations. Organizations assessing their task as "Q" may be employed for those tasks. The unit possesses the necessary resources or those resources have been explicitly identified to the organization to allow it to execute when ordered.

    c. <u>No "N" Assessment</u>. The organization is unable to accomplish the task to standard at this time.

6. <u>Required Remarks</u>. If any METs are assessed as "No", explain the capability shortfall, as well as the resources, training, or forces required to resolve the shortfall. Address any standards assessed as not meeting required criteria. EXAMPLE: "80% TRAINED TO STANDARD, NOT ABLE TO TRAIN TO AMPHIB OPS UNTIL DEC WHEN AMPHIB SHIPS AVAIL. ABLE PERFORM AMPHIP PORTION OF MSN AFTER THIS TRNG."

Chapter 5

Training

1. <u>Purpose</u>. This chapter outlines policy for reporting training (T-rating).

2. <u>Policy</u>. The T-rating is one of the four measured areas that are factors in determining a unit's C-level. The determination of a T-level will be based on the unit's present state, not a future projection.

3. <u>Scope</u>. T-ratings will be calculated only by units (including intermediate level commands), not by installations or MARFORs.

4. <u>Training (T-Rating)</u>. The T-rating is an assessment of the unit's training to accomplish its designed mission.

a. Units, to include intermediate level units, will base their T-rating on the percentage of their core METs trained to standard using Table 5-1 as a reference. For example, if a battalion was trained to standard in four of its five METs, it would have a T-rating of T-2 (80%).

Table 5-1.—-T-Rating Calculation

Rule	T1	T2	T3	T4
Percentage of Core METs Trained to Standard	≥85%	70-84%	55-69%	<55%

b. <u>Aviation Units</u>. For aviation units guided by references (i) through (k), the T-rating reported will be the lower of the Combat Leadership assessment or the Training Percentage.

5. <u>Mandatory Training Remarks</u>. Report the exact percentage of METs trained to standard, list the METs not trained to standard and their impact on readiness, and provide amplifying remarks outlining the support needed to improve training. EXAMPLE: "80% TRAINED TO STANDARD, NOT ABLE TO TRAIN TO AMPHIB OPS UNTIL DEC WHEN AMPHIB SHIPS AVAIL. ABLE PERFORM AMPHIP PORTION OF MSN AFTER THIS TRNG."

6. <u>Training Reason Codes</u>. Enter the Training Reason Codes from Appendix G, Table G-1 to explain the unit's T-rating when it is less than 1.

Enclosure (1)

Chapter 6

Chemical, Biological, Radiological, and Nuclear (CBRN) Defense

1. Purpose. This Chapter outlines policy for reporting CBRN Defense readiness.

2. Policy. Reference (a) requires unit commanders to provide a subjective assessment of their unit's readiness to accomplish its mission under CBRN conditions. The CBRN Defense assessment is a separate assessment based on the reported levels of CBRN equipment and training. As a separate reporting requirement, the CBRN Defense assessment does not directly influence or contribute to a unit's overall C-level calculations; however, a commander may subjectively change the unit's overall reported C-level and core mission assessment when a CBRN deficiency or asset directly impacts the unit's ability to carry out its wartime mission. CBRN will be assessed in each readiness report.

3. Scope. This Chapter pertains to units. Installations and MARFORs will not report CBRN defense readiness.

4. Reporting Requirements. CBRN Defense readiness policy is explained in this chapter. Guidance on reporting procedures, mandatory remarks, and reason codes are contained in Appendix D.

   a. Overall CBRN Level. Units will determine the Overall CBRN Level based on reported ratings of CBRN defense equipment and CBRN training. The Overall CBRN Level will not be higher than the lowest of the ratings for CBRN defense equipment and CBRN training.

   b. CBRN Defense Equipment (S-rating). Marine Corps CBRN defense equipment is managed by MARCORSYSCOM as a Centrally Managed Program under the Program Manager for Combat Support Equipment (PM CSE). PM CSE is responsible for ensuring the Marine Corps CBRN equipment inventory is sufficient to support readiness. PM CSE assesses the Marine Corps CBRN equipment for deficiencies and coordinates all readiness issues with DC PP&O (POR) and DC CD&I. DC CD&I is the Marine Corps' Advocate for CBRN Defense. MARCORLOGCOM stores, maintains and issues the Marine Corps' CBRN equipment within the Consolidated Storage Program (CSP) at distributed Unit Issue Facilities (UIF) and Individual Issue Facilities (IIF). The Marine Corps' Centralized Management of CBRN defense equipment eliminated the unit commanders' responsibility to fund for and sustain CBRN defense equipment. When shortages exist, the consolidation of CBRN equipment within the CSP allows the Marine Corps to rapidly shift CBRN assets to support deploying units. This ability to support units from a centralized pool of equipment ensures deploying units are fully equipped with the best CBRN equipment in the inventory. Garrison units should request equipment data for their CBRN equipment rating from the CBRN officer or staff noncommissioned officer within the chain of command. Determine the CBRN equipment rating using the procedures in Appendix D and Table 6-1.

Table 6-1.--CBRN Defense Equipment S-Rating

Rule	S1	S2	S3	S4
Aggregate average of total serviceable selected CBRN Equipment possessed divided by total required quantity	90-100%	80-89%	65-79%	0-65%

c. <u>CBRN Defense Training (T-rating)</u>. CBRN training requirements are per references (e), (l), and (m). The CBRN T-rating is an assessment of the unit's training to accomplish its designed mission under CBRN conditions. It considers the accomplishment of required individual and unit training. All units will base their CBRN T-rating on the percentage of their core METs trained to standard under CBRN conditions within the past 12 months. Determine the CBRN T-rating using the procedures in Appendix D and Table 6-2.

Table 6-2.--CBRN Defense Training T-Rating

Rule	T1	T2	T3	T4
Percentage of METs Trained to Standard under CBRN conditions in the past 12 months	85-100%	70-84%	55-69%	0-55%

Chapter 7

Commander's Assessments

1. <u>Purpose</u>. This chapter outlines policy for the Commander's readiness assessment of his/her organization.

2. <u>Policy</u>. The commander's assessments encompass the C-level and capability assessments for the organization's core mission, as well as the PCTEF and capability assessments for assigned mission(s). The commander's assessments will be based on the organization's present state, not a future projection. Remarks will provide additional information, such as projected changes in readiness.

3. <u>Scope</u>. C-level and PCTEF will be calculated only by units (including intermediate level commands), not installations or MARFORs All Marine Corps readiness reporting organization commanders will make capability assessments of their core and assigned missions.

4. <u>Reporting Requirements</u>. Policy regarding the commander's assessments is explained in this chapter. Reporting procedures, guidance, mandatory remarks, and reason codes for the Commander's assessments are contained in Appendix E. The operational readiness of Marine Corps organizations is directly impacted by their capabilities, resourcing, and training. Accurate assessments by commanders are essential for helping the Marine Corps, combatant commands, and the Department of Defense understand their capability to accomplish tactical, operational, and strategic goals.

   a. <u>C-Level Assessment</u>

      (1) The C-level reflects the status of the selected unit resources measured against the resources required to undertake the core mission for which the unit is task organized or designed. The C-level also reflects the condition of available equipment, personnel, and unit training status. C-levels, by themselves, do not project a unit's combat performance once committed to combat. The five C-levels and their definitions are listed in Table E-1. Units will not report C-5, unless directed to do so by DC PP&O.

      (2) The overall C-level will equate to the lowest rating of any of the unit's individually measured resource and training ratings (P, R, S or T).

(3) <u>C-5 Level Ratings</u>

(a) The exception to the above policy is for units reporting C-5. C-5 is used for units undergoing CMC directed resource actions and the changes in their resource and training ratings (P, S, R, and T) should be tracked with the appropriate numeric ratings of 1 through 4.

(b) Units reporting C-5 will remain C-5 until all ratings (P, S, R, and T) are 3 or higher, unless directed otherwise by PP&O, POR. A rating of C-5 does not prevent the deployment of ready detachments from the unit.

(4) <u>Subjective C-Level Changes</u>

(a) The commander may subjectively raise or lower the C-level. In determining the need for a subjective upgrade or downgrade of the C-level, the commander will determine whether the subjectively changed C-level would be in consonance with the C-level definitions listed in Appendix E, Table E-1. For instance, units missing important personnel or equipment should be guarded against a subjective upgrade to C-1.

(b) A subjective change of the C-level does not permit a change to the resource and training ratings (P, R, S and T). They will be reported without adjustment.

(c) A subjective change of the C-level results in the requirement to submit a Reason Code (Appendix E, Table E-2) and a mandatory remark.

(5) <u>Forecast C-level and Date.</u> The commander will report any forecasted increase or decrease in the unit's C-level with the date of the forecasted change. Remarks explaining the projected increase or decrease in readiness are required. Explain why, if a forecasted change or date is not possible.

(6) <u>C-Level and Core Mission Capability Assessments.</u> These assessments should correlate. Appendix E, Table E-3 provides guidance.

(7) C-Level Reason Codes and mandatory remarks are contained in Appendix E. Remarks are required for all C-level assessments.

b. PCTEF Assessment. PCTEF ratings are calculated like C-level ratings. PCTEF levels and their definitions are contained in Table E-4.

(1) A commander's evaluation of the unit's ability to perform the assigned mission cannot be based solely on P, S, R, and T-ratings. The cumulative effect of these measured areas, with other important factors, could have a positive or negative implication on the unit's ability to execute its assigned mission. For the commander to assess the unit's current military capability to respond to the full spectrum of designated mission requirements, the commander must consider additional factors. Although not all inclusive, other factors for the commander to consider are: personnel turnover, availability of ranges and training areas, installation support, operational tempo, exercises, and leadership.

(2) If the unit has more than one assigned mission, then the assigned mission the unit is focusing on for training and execution will be the basis for the PCTEF assessment.

(3) The PCTEF assessment will not necessarily correlate with the unit's overall C-level. For instance, if an infantry battalion is assigned a humanitarian assistance mission, PCTEF will capture an assessment against the humanitarian assistance mission while the overall C-level will assess the unit's ability to execute its core mission. If the assigned mission is the same as the core mission, the C-level and PCTEF assessments should be the same.

(4) PCTEF reporting occasions are shown in Table 1-1.

(5) The PCTEF level should correlate with capability assessments for assigned missions as depicted in Appendix E, Table E-3.

c. Core and Assigned Mission Capability Assessments

(1) Commanders will assess the capability of their organizations to execute their core and assigned (OPLAN/CONPLAN and Named Operation) missions using a Yes (Y), Qualified Yes (Q), and No (N) criteria based on their assessed METs for those missions. The mission assessments will consider the missions as a whole and should reflect the Commander's military experience and judgment on all the tasks and factors that affect the organization's ability to meet mission objectives. Table E-5

contains the definitions and guidelines for the Y, Q, and N mission assessment criteria.

(2) Core and assigned mission capability assessments should align respectively with C-Level and PCTEF assessments as depicted in Appendix E, Table E-3.

5. <u>Guided Remarks</u>. If not stated in other remarks, Commanders should provide amplifying remarks for the following instances to assist with resourcing, training, and force management decisions:

a. <u>Change in C-Level and/or PCTEF Since Last Report</u>. Explain what caused the change since the last report.

b. Identify key readiness degraders within each section of the report (Personnel, Equipment, Training, CBRN, etc).

c. State what actions are being taken to mitigate readiness degraders.

d. State what assistance is needed from higher headquarters.

Appendix A

Personnel Procedures

1. <u>Purpose</u>. This appendix provides the procedures to calculate personnel readiness. Policy information on personnel readiness is contained in Chapter 2.

2. <u>Assembly of Personnel Information</u>. Personnel information should be consolidated by the personnel officer (G-1/S-1) and provided to the Marine assembling the readiness report. The completion of a personnel worksheet is recommended prior to starting the report. Samples of personnel worksheets are contained in Appendix F.

3. <u>Personnel Location</u>. Personnel locations will be reported using standard geographical location (GEOLOC) codes or ship UICs for personnel embarked aboard ships. Units with assigned personnel at more than one location will report the personnel data for each geographic location.

4. <u>Type Personnel Codes (TPERS)</u>. Personnel are reported by type codes as defined in Table G-3. Use the same code (MC) for commissioned and warrant officers. Refer to the glossary in Appendix I for definitions of personnel reporting terms.

5. <u>Personnel Adjustments for Task Organization</u>. The policy for personnel adjustments of assigned and structured quantities is provided in paragraph 6, chapter 2, in this Order. Task organized units gaining personnel will add assigned strength, structured strength, and MOS Fill quantities. The Assigned Strength and MOS Fill quantities will be subtracted from the providing unit(s). Figure A-1 provides an example of these adjustments with an artillery battalion providing a battery of 134 personnel to form a battalion landing team.

Figure A-1.—-Personnel Task Organization Adjustments

Prior to Task Organization				
Artillery Battalion				Infantry Battalion
$\frac{550}{600}$	=	Assigned Strength Structured Strength	=	748 760

After Task Organization

A battery of 134 Marines and Sailors detached to the battalion landing team

Artillery Battalion				Battalion Landing Team
$\frac{416}{600}$	=	Assigned Strength Structured Strength	=	882 894

6. <u>Mandatory Personnel Remarks</u>. Mandatory remarks and examples are:

     a. <u>Assigned Strength (ASGD) Remark</u>. Identify changes due to assigned strength. **EXAMPLE REMARK OF UNIT PROVIDING PERSONNEL**: "ASGD Bn decreased by detaching B Battery to BLT 1/2; 7/125/0/2 MC/ME/NC/NE".

     b. <u>Structure Strength (STRUC) Remark</u>. Identify changes due to structure strength. **EXAMPLE REMARK OF TASK ORGANIZED UNIT GAINING PERSONNEL**: "BLT STRUC increased by attaching a battery from 1/10; to 1/2; 7/125/0/2 MC/ME/NC/NE".

     c. <u>Critical MOSs</u>. Identify the three critical PMOSs that have the largest detrimental impact on the unit's readiness and explain why they were selected and the impact they have. Up to ten primary MOSs can be entered as critical MOSs in DRRS-MC.

     d. <u>P-Level is Not 1</u>. Explain why and the impact. EXAMPLE REMARK: "Detached a battery to 1/2 and cannot fully support an infantry regiment with fire support."

     e. <u>Employed/Deployed Personnel</u>. State the percentage of personnel employed or deployed when five percent (5%) or more of a unit's personnel are detached to another unit.

7. <u>Personnel Reason Codes</u>. Enter the Personnel Reason Codes from Table G-1 to explain the unit's status when the P-level is less than 1.

8. <u>Employ/Deploy Codes</u>. If these codes were used, state the percentage of personnel employed/deployed to other units.

Appendix B

Equipment Procedures

1. <u>Purpose</u>. This appendix provides procedures, guidance, mandatory remarks, and reason codes for reporting equipment. Policy information on equipment readiness is contained in Chapter 3.

2. <u>Assembly of Equipment Information</u>. Equipment information should be consolidated by the Logistics Officer (G-4/S-4) with the support of the supply and maintenance officers. The completion of an equipment worksheet is recommended prior to starting the report.

3. <u>MEE Location</u>. MEE located away from the unit will have its quantities and location reported. Report the location using standard geographical location (GEOLOC) codes or ship UICs for equipment embarked aboard ships.

4. <u>Equipment Adjustments for Task Organization: S-Ratings</u>. The policy for materiel adjustments of possessed and prescribed wartime requirement quantities is provided in Chapter 3, paragraph 8 in this Order. The task organized units receiving equipment will add the possessed and prescribed wartime requirement quantities. The units providing the equipment to the task organized unit will subtract only the possessed quantities, not the prescribed wartime requirement quantities. Figure B-1 provides an example of these adjustments with an artillery battalion providing a battery of 6 howitzers to form a battalion landing team. The same procedure would be followed to illustrate an aviation unit chopping aircraft to support a MEU deployment.

5. <u>Mandatory Equipment Remarks</u>. Mandatory remarks and examples are:

   a. <u>S and/or R-Rating Not 1</u>. Explain why, what the impact is on the unit's mission(s), what is being done to correct the problem and what assistance is required. EXAMPLE: MALS-XX HAS ONLY 70% OF ITS IMRL; REMAINDER SHIPPED TO OEF. CRITICAL IMRL GEAR COMING FROM MALS-YY BY 1 DEC, WHICH WILL ENABLE UNIT TO PROVIDE MINIMAL SUPPORT TO MAG."

   b. <u>Aircraft Out of Reporting Status</u>. State the quantities and status. EXAMPLE: "2 ACFT AT SDLM, 1 ACFT AT MALS FOR DEPOT REPAIR."

c. Reserve Units' Training Allowances (T/A). Selected Marine Corps Reserve units will report the percentage of their T/A that is on-hand. This calculation is not the same as the S-rating.

Figure B-1.--Equipment Task Organization Adjustments

Prior to Task Organization		
Artillery Battalion		Infantry Battalion

$$\frac{18 \text{ howitzers}}{18 \text{ howitzers}} = \frac{\text{Possessed}}{\text{Prescribed wartime requirement}} = \frac{0}{0}$$

After Task Organization

A battery of howitzers detached to the battalion landing team

Artillery Battalion			Battalion Landing Team

$$\frac{12}{18} = \frac{\text{Possessed}}{\text{Prescribed wartime Requirement}} = \frac{6}{6}$$

6. Equipment Reason Codes. Enter the Equipment Reason Codes from Appendix G, Table G-1 to explain the unit's status when the S and/or R-rating are not 1.

7. Employ/Deploy Codes. If these codes were used, state the percentage of equipment employed/deployed to other units.

Appendix C

MET Assessment

1. Purpose. This appendix provides the procedures to assess
METs. Policy information on MET assessments is provided in
Chapter 4.

2. Assembly of Information. MET assessment information should
be consolidated by the Operations Officer (G-3/S-3), with the
support of the Personnel (G-1/S-1), Squadron Maintenance
Department, and Logistics (G-4/S-4) Officers to provide resource
information regarding MET conditions.

3. MET Assessment Guidance. Guidance on the MET assessment
definitions is listed below and depicted in Figure C-1. Based
on the commander's assessment of MET performance standards, the
commander will conduct his MET Assessment by checking Resourced,
Trained, and Observed as appropriate. The relationship between
these three selections will drive the MET Assessment of Y/Q/N.

   a. Resourced. The organization meets standards for
personnel, equipment, and subordinate forces for the task. The
resources are in possession or have been explicitly identified
to the organization to allow it to execute when ordered.

   b. Trained. The organization meets established training
standards for the task.

   c. Observed. The organization has demonstrated, in
training or operations, the ability to produce the task's output
measures to standard. An organization observed successfully
meeting MET performance standards will be considered, and
marked, "Trained" during the MET assessment.

Table C-1.-—MET Assessment Guidance

Resourced	Trained	Observed	MET Assessment (Y=Yes, Q=Qualified Yes, N=No)
√	√	√	Y
√	√		Q
√			N
	√	√	Q
	√		N
			N

Appendix D

Chemical, Biological, Radiological, and Nuclear Defense (CBRN)
Readiness Reporting Procedures

1. Purpose. This appendix provides procedures, mandatory remarks, and reason codes used to calculate and report CBRN defense readiness. Policy on CBRN defense is provided in Chapter 6.

2. Procedures. Commanders will assess the availability and condition of equipment and unit training conducted as it pertains to CBRN Defense. The unit CBRN Defense Officer/Chief is responsible for advising the Commander on the unit's CBRN readiness level and for calculating the CBRN S-rating, T-rating and Overall C-level. Remarks are required for all CBRN C-levels to clarify the Commander's assessment. As applicable, a forecast improvement/downturn date, reason codes, and remarks will accompany the assessment when the assessment is made and the S-rating or T-rating are not 1.

3. CBRN Defense Equipment (S-Rating). The CBRN Equipment Worksheet found in Appendix F is used to determine the CBRN equipment S-rating. These steps will help with completing the worksheet.

   a. Data. Two data elements are required to complete the worksheet;

      (1) Unit's Approved Acquisition Objective (AAO) For Applicable Items. The Unit AAO can be found in the unit's Table of Organization and Equipment (TO&E) for the current fiscal year as maintained in the Total Force Structure Management System (TFSMS). The AAO column in TFSMS will be changed to read the Unit T/E Requirement (UTR).

      (2) Quantity of Serviceable CBRN Equipment On-hand.

   b. CBRN Readiness Calculator. A CBRN Readiness Calculator that greatly reduces the time required to determine the CBRN Equipment rating, eliminates the need to perform manual calculations, and provides the same results as the Worksheet is maintained by Marine Corps Systems Command and is available for use at https://ips.usmc.mil/sites/mcsccbrn/default.aspx. It is recommended for use due to its efficiency and because its equipment data is kept current.

c. Worksheet Procedures. Manual procedures for the CBRN Equipment Rating Worksheet follow.

(1) Authorized Column. Record the Unit AAO Quantities from the TFSMS generated unit TO&E report for the current FY.

(2) Serviceable-On Hand Column. Record the actual quantity of serviceable equipment the unit has on hand to include equipment issued to individuals in the unit.

(3) Percent On Hand Column. Calculate the Percent On Hand for each item as follows; "Authorized" divided by "Serviceable On Hand" equals the "Percent On Hand". Round to nearest whole number. For example; 90 divided by 100 equals 0.9 or 90%.

(4) Rating Column. Apply the appropriate rating from Table 6-1.

(5) Overall CBRN Sense Rating. The overall CBRN Sense rating is the average of four Sense capability area ratings: Chemical Detection Rating, Biological Detection Rating, Radiological/Nuclear Detection Rating, and CBRN Detection Equipment Rating. Spaces are provided on the worksheet to record the four Sense capability area ratings and the Overall CBRN Sense Rating.

(a) Chemical Detection Rating. Determine the number by averaging the chemical detection equipment ratings from the Rating Column.

(b) Biological Detection Rating. The Marine Corps has not fielded a biological detection capability, so there are no AAOs for such equipment loaded in TFSMS. Units will enter "4" in the space provided, until the Marine Corps requirement for a biological detection system has been met.

(c) Radiological/Nuclear Detection Rating. Determine the number by averaging the radiological/nuclear detection equipment ratings from the Rating Column.

(d) CBRN Detection Rating. Determine the number by averaging the CBRN detection equipment ratings from the Rating Column.

(6) <u>CBRN Shield Overall Rating</u>. The rating is based on separate assessments of Ground and Aviation CBRN defense equipment. It is the lower of the Ground Equipment Rating or the Aviation Equipment Rating, which are described below.

(a) <u>Ground Equipment Rating</u>. Average all the ratings in the Rating Column under Ground Equipment. Compare the average ground equipment rating to the ground equipment ratings for the equipment identified with an asterisk. The equipment associated with the asterisks directly support individual survival in a CBRN environment. A shortage of any one of the items with an asterisk will reduce the overall S-rating to no higher than the lowest asterisk rating. Enter the lowest rating from the average rating for the ground equipment or the asterisk ratings in the space provided for the overall Ground Equipment Rating.

(b) <u>Aviation Equipment Rating</u>. This equipment is managed by the Navy and there are no AAOs. So the CBRN equipment required to support aircrews must be a subjective assessment. If the Aviation Equipment Rating is lower than the ground equipment rating, the lower rating will be entered in the space provided for the Subjective S-rating.

(7) <u>CBRN Sustain Rating</u>. Calculate the rating column for each piece of equipment and determine their average. Compare this average to the sustain equipment ratings for the asterisk items. If any of the asterisk ratings are lower than the average, the lowest asterisk rating is used for the overall CBRN Sustain Rating. If none of the asterisk ratings are lower than the sustain equipment average, the average is used for the overall CBRN Sustain Rating. The asterisk equipment directly support individual survival in a CBRN environment. A shortage of any one of these items will reduce the overall S-rating to no higher than the lowest asterisk rating.

(8) <u>CBRN Medical</u>. The Medical Logistics (MedLog) Companies are the only units that report CBRN medical readiness while in garrison.

(a) Calculate the Percent On Hand for each item. The CBRN Medical Rating will be the average of the three items, unless one of the asterisk items is lower. If the latter occurs, use the lowest highlighted rating.

(b) Deploying units report CBRN medical readiness when they draw their Authorized Medical Allowance List (AMAL) from MedLog. Such units will subjectively assess their CBRN medical items when deployed to a CBRN threat area and enter that subjective assessment in the space provided for the CBRN Medical Subjective Rating.

        (9) <u>CBRN Equipment Rating</u>. Average the four CBRN Capability Area Ratings: CBRN Sense, CBRN Shape, CBRN Shield, CBRN Sustain, and CBRN Medical. Compare the average rating to the overall CBRN Shield Rating. The lower of the two ratings is the CBRN Equipment Rating. Enter the CBRN Equipment Rating in the space provided at the top of the worksheet under Calculated.

        (10) <u>Subjective Ratings</u>. When the individual preparing the worksheet believes the calculated ratings do not accurately reflect the unit's CBRN equipment readiness, the Subjective Ratings should be filled in for CBRN Sense, CBRN Shape, CBRN Shield, CBRN Sustain, CBRN Medical, and the CBRN Equipment S-Rating. The unit commander will decide whether to report the calculated or subjective ratings.

4. <u>CBRN Defense Training (T-Rating)</u>. The CBRN T-rating is determined in the same manner as the T-rating described in Chapter 5, paragraph 4 for all core METs trained for CBRN conditions within the past 12 months. Accomplishment of required individual and unit CBRN training will be considered when applying the subjective rating.

5. <u>CBRN Defense Overall Readiness Level</u>. The lower of the CBRN Defense Equipment and CBRN Defense Training ratings is used for the Overall CBRN Defense Readiness level. Provide a reason code from Appendix G when the overall CBRN level is not CBRN-1.

6. <u>CBRN Forecast</u>. The commander will state in the remarks a forecasted improvement/downturn date when the overall CBRN rating is less than CBRN-1 and briefly explain what is required to return the unit to CBRN-1. When determining an improvement/downturn date is not possible, state so and provide the reason why.

Appendix E

Commander's Assessment Procedures

1. <u>Purpose</u>. This appendix provides reporting procedures, guidance, reason codes, and mandatory remarks for reporting the Commander's assessments. Policy information on Commanders' assessments is contained in Chapter 7.

2. <u>Reporting Procedures</u>

a. <u>C-Level Assessment</u>. The five C-levels and their definitions are listed in Table E-1. Units will not report C-5, unless directed to do so by DC PP&O or a Marine Corps Bulletin 5400.

Table E-1.—C-Level Definitions

C-Level	Definition
C-1	The unit possesses the required resources and is trained to undertake the <u>full</u> wartime mission(s) for which it is organized or designed. The resource and training area status will neither limit flexibility in methods for mission accomplishment nor increase vulnerability of unit personnel and equipment. The unit does not require any compensation for deficiencies.
C-2	The unit possesses the required resources and is trained to undertake <u>most</u> of the wartime mission(s) for which it is organized or designed. The resource and training area status may cause isolated decreases in flexibility in methods for mission accomplishment, but will not increase vulnerability of the unit under most envisioned operational scenarios. The unit would require little, if any, compensation for deficiencies.
C-3	The unit possesses the required resources and is trained to undertake <u>many, but not all, portions</u> of the wartime mission(s) for which it is organized or designed. The resource or training area status will result in significant decreases in flexibility for mission accomplishment and will increase vulnerability of the unit under many, but not all, envisioned operational scenarios. The unit would require significant compensation for deficiencies.
C-4	The unit <u>requires additional resources</u> or training to undertake its wartime mission(s), but it may be directed to undertake portions of its wartime mission(s) with resources on hand.

C-5	The unit is undertaking a CMC-directed resource action and is not prepared, at this time, to undertake the wartime mission(s) for which it is organized or designed.

(1) C-Level Reason Codes. A C-level reason code is mandatory when the C-level is not 1 or when the Commander subjectively changes the unit C-level per his/her judgment. The "X" code for a Subjective C-level change has precedence over the other codes and should be used first, if applicable. These codes are contained in Table E-2.

Table E-2.--C-Level Reason Codes

CODE	DEFINITION
P	Personnel
S	Equipment and Supplies On-hand
R	Equipment Condition
T	Training
X	Commander's Subjective Judgment (Explanatory remarks are required.)
N	Not Available (CMC directed)

(2) Assessment Correlation. Use Table E-3 to ensure that C-level and PCTEF assessments correlate respectively with core and assigned mission capability assessments.

Table E-3.--Assessment Correlation

C-Level/ PCTEF	Mission Capability Assessment
C-1	Y or Q
C-2	Y or Q
C-3	N
C-4	N
C-5	N

b. PCTEF Assessment

(1) Calculating Resource and Training Ratings. These ratings will be calculated in the same manner as the ratings for a C-level. Chapter 2 addresses personnel ratings, Chapter 3 addresses equipment ratings, and Chapter 5 addresses training ratings.

(2) <u>PCTEF Levels</u>. Table E-4 contains definitions for the different PCTEF levels. PCTEF does not have a level 5.

Table E-4.--PCTEF Definitions

PCTEF Level	PCTEF Definitions
1	Unit has full flexibility and will not need extraordinary assistance to carry out mission.
2	Unit may encounter isolated decreases in Flexibility, but vulnerability will usually be acceptable relative to mission criticality.
3	Unit will encounter significant decreases in flexibility and increased vulnerability may be unacceptable relative to mission criticality.
4	Mission success is possible for certain isolated scenarios, but flexibility will be severely restricted.

c. <u>Core and Assigned Mission Capability Assessments</u>. These assessments will be made using a Yes (Y), Qualified Yes (Q), and No (N) criteria. The definition of that criteria and the guidance for assignment are contained in Table E-5.

Table E-5.--Mission Capability Assessment Guidance

Assessment	Definition	Guidance
Yes (Y)	The organization can accomplish the mission to conditions and prescribed standards	The majority of the METs are assessed as Yes and the remaining METs are assessed as Qualified Yes
Qualified Yes (Q)	The organization can accomplish the mission to standard under most conditions, but this performance has not been observed or demonstrated in training or operations. A "Qualified yes" equates to a "Yes" in that it sends the message the organization is prepared to conduct the mission under the prescribed conditions and standards.	The majority of the METs are assessed as Qualified Yes and the remaining METs are assessed as Yes
No (N)	The organization cannot accomplish the mission to	A No MET assessment will normally preclude a

	the standards and conditions prescribed	mission assessment of Yes. The Commander must make a judgment if the mission can still be accomplished if a MET is assessed as No

3. <u>Mandatory Remarks</u>. General remarks required of all C-level, PCTEF, core, and assigned mission capability assessments to help higher headquarters understand the organization's mission, readiness, and capabilities. Remarks specific to certain assessments are listed below.

    a. <u>General</u>

        (1) The Commander's remarks should explain, in succinct and easily understood terms, the "bottom line" assessment of organization's capability to carry out its missions. This is especially important for intermediate commands, which must not simply repeat data and remarks from subordinate units.

        (2) Identify changes to the unit's tasking, organization, or renaming of the unit due to operational requirements. EXAMPLE: "3RD MAR REGT REDESIGNATED AS SP MAGTF A."

        (3) Describe readiness issues in sufficient detail to support corrective action and prioritization of resources. Key information needed from each Commander are resources and capabilities needed for the unit to be a 1 or Y and length of time required to train to the unit's METs once the resources are on hand.

        (4) Intermediate level units will highlight subordinate unit issues and shortfalls and state actions taken to assist them.

    b. <u>C-Level and PCTEF Remarks</u>

        (1) <u>When the C-Level/PCTEF Is Other Than 1</u>. Clarify impact the resource and training ratings have on the ability of the unit to carry out its core and assigned missions.

        (2) <u>Forecast C-Level/PCTEF Changes</u>. State the dates when the C-level and/or PCTEF are anticipated to change, state why, and state the predicted level (1-5).

(3) <u>C-5 Units</u>.   State why the unit is C-5.

(4) <u>Subjective Change in C-Level</u>.   Identify the reason and provide supporting comments.

(5) Units with remain behind personnel and/or equipment will explain the impact on the core mission.

(6) State the P, S, R, and T ratings for the PCTEF assessment.

Appendix F

Worksheets

1. <u>Purpose</u>. This appendix provides worksheets to assist with assembling a readiness report. Their use is optional.

2. <u>Personnel Worksheet</u>. It should be the responsibility of the unit's Personnel Section (S-1) to provide an accurate worksheet. Guidance for completing this work sheet, Figure F-1 is:

    a. <u>Use Current Fiscal Year T/O to Determine Structure Strength</u>. Use the current fiscal year T/O from the TFSMS to analyze the T/O and document correct quantities for each type personnel (TPERS) (see Table G-3). Enter the T/O unit identification code and fiscal year on the worksheet.

    b. <u>Determine Assigned Strength by Person</u>. Each person assigned to the unit will fill a T/O billet per TPERS; for example 30/165/1/5 means 30 MC, 165 ME, 1 NC, and 5 NE. This is the Assigned Strength. Align each person to a specific T/O line number by MOS, one up or one down in rank, if in the same MOS.

    c. <u>Determine the Unit's Task Organization</u>. Subtract or add to STRUC and ASGD by TPERS. Enter unit STRUC numbers on worksheet with the geolocation code and the correct STRUC and ASGD mandatory remarks.

    d. <u>IAs, and JMDs</u>. Subtract these personnel from the ASGD strength only, because they are considered not available for deployment with the parent unit.

    e. Make the STRUC numbers the second entry requirement on the worksheet. Then account for these with correct STRUC and ASGD remarks for task organization. These remarks must be accurate and formatted properly to capture task organization impacts.

    f. Determine the non-deployables by TPERS (Table G-3) and the reasons codes (Table G-5). Total by TPERS and place in the Non-Deployable column at the present location code (PRGEO) TPERS locations. Place Non-Deployable numbers by category in the column; Legal, Admin, etc.

g. Determine how many locations are active for training or other missions for unit personnel. Make the appropriate geolocation Code entries for affected TPERS under the first entered geolocation in the location column.

h. Determine how many of each TPERS are at each PEGEO location. Make the appropriate number entries by TPERS for each location listed under MC/ME/NC/NE. Subtract these from the ASGD totals by TPERS arrived at in step "b". Assume all personnel at away locations are deployable and MOS qualified, subtracting the away assigned number equally from the deployed and MOS-Fill totals respectively. <u>After all locations are subtracted</u>, what remains should be the correct number of personnel assigned for each PRGEO TPERS "ASGD" and MOS-Fill entry.

i. Subtract each TPERS non-deployable total from the remaining PRGEO ASGD numbers. The remaining number represents the number for each TPERS category that is entered into the Deployable column.

j. Using the TPERS totals for MOS-Fill, subtract away location numbers from each PRGEO TPERS. The remaining number is entered into the appropriate PRGEO TPERS in the MOS-Fill column.

k. Add each column and determine unit totals for STRUC, ASGD, Deployable, Non-Deployable and MOS-Fill. These should match the original totals. If not, find the error in math.

l. Discuss with the S-1 section what MOS' have the largest operational impact of those shortages to determine which MOS' should be categorized as "Critical." Enter these in the worksheet space.

m. Using the totals, determine the P-Rating (per Figure 2-1 and Table 2-1). If not P-1, determine the correct Personnel reason code and recommended mandatory remarks from the S-1. The worksheet should now be complete, accurate, and telling the personnel "rest of the story."

Figure F-1.--Personnel Worksheet

USMC PERSONNEL WORKSHEET

TPERS	GEO LOC	STRUC	ASGD	DEPLOY	NON-DEPLOY	MOS FILL	T/O NUMBER	T/O DTE
MC								
ME								
NC								
NE								
TOTALS								

DEPLOYABLE STRENGTH

MC	ME	NC	NE

MOS FILL TOTALS BY TPERS

MC	ME	NC	NE

CROSS CHECK FIGURES: ASGD = DEPLOYABLE + NON DEPLOYABLE:

STRUC = T/O (+) OR (-) ADJUSTMENTS

CRITICAL MOS'S: Mandatory

MOS	STRUC	ON HAND

NON-DEPLOYABLES

	MC	ME	NC	NE
ADMIN				
LEGAL				
MEDICAL				
MOS				
CC				
OTHER				

NOTE: MOS fill will only include personnel which possess MOS of T/O billet assigned.

SORTS MANDATORY REMARKS:

REQUIRED FOR EACH REPORT WHILE THESE REMAIN Attached or Detached.

Ex: "INCREASED OR DECREASED FROM OR TO UNIT BY MC/ME/NC/NE" I.E. INCREASED 2/15/0/1 FM 2D LAR

OR "DECREASED BY 2/20/0/1 TO MSSG-22."

STRUC: _____

ASGD: _____

PEGEO: Temp location by TPERS MC/ME/NC/NE

P-RATING:_____ (SORTS Generated- Fill and Sheet is CLASSIFIED)

NOTE: MANDATORY REASON CODE IF UNIT IS NOT C-1.

PRRES RSN	DESCRIPTION

MANDATORY/REGULAR REMARK: PRRES - PROVIDE DETAILS ON REASON (S) FOR DEGRADATION.

(DO NOT USE THE REASON CODE DESCRIPTIONS)

_____

ADMINISTRATIVE OFFICER   DATE

3. <u>Equipment Worksheet</u>. It should be the responsibility of the unit's Logistics Section (S-4) to provide an accurate worksheet. Guidance for completing this work sheet, Figure F-2 is:

a.   S-Rating

        (1) Rollup on TAMCN (ROT). ROT occurs when "S"
ratings are calculated for individual TAMCNs at any
organizational level. For individual TAMCNs, net excess
(possessed quantities above the wartime requirement) is
subtracted from the possessed quantity when determining the
numerator for calculating the "S" rating. Note:
Quantities above the wartime requirement will be annotated
in DRRS-MC under the column "EXCESS." The EXCESS data is
informational only and not used to calculate the S-rating.

        (2) Rollup Across TAMCNs (RAT). RAT occurs when
"S" ratings are calculated for multiple TAMCNs. When
calculating "S" ratings across TAMCNs, excesses for one
TAMCN must not compensate for deficiencies in other TAMCNs,
since including excesses would artificially inflate the "S"
rating. Before calculating "S" ratings across TAMCNs,
individual TAMCN excesses must be computed using the ROT
rule. The individual TAMCN net excess' are added, and the
sum of all net-excess for all TAMCNs is subtracted from the
total on-hand of all TAMCNs being computed to determine the
numerator for computing the "s" rating across TAMCNs. The
formula is: On-hand minus net excess divided by
requirement.

        (3) The second step is to compare the MEE and PEI
percentages derived in the first step. Units will select
the S-rating for the designated MEE or selected PEI with
the lowest percentage (see Table 3-1).

    b.   Equipment Condition (R-rating) Computations.
Chapter 3 and Appendix B outline equipment condition
calculations and associated status rating. The R-rating is
computed separately for MEE and PEI items. Computation
steps are:

        (1) Subtract the total number of dead-lined items
from the total number of possessed (in reporting status)
items.

        (2) Divide the above quantity by the total
possessed (in reporting status) quantity of items (see
Table 3-2).

(3) Compare the percentages for MEE and PEI derived in steps (1) and (2) and use the lowest one to determine the R-rating per Table 3-2.

Figure F-2.—Equipment Worksheet

USMC EQUIPMENT WORKSHEET

MISSION ESSENTIAL EQUIPMENT (MEE)

T/E AUTHORIZED (MEPSA) ONLY REPORT AT THE Hqtrs (PRGEO) location.

		MEPSA	MEPSD			MEORC	UNIT TOT%	UNIT TOT%		
MEPT ID	GEO LOC	T/E AUTH	POSS'D	EXCESS	D/LINED	OP RDY	MEPSA	MEORC	T/E NBR	T/E DATE
TOTALS		0	0	0	0	0				

ALL TYPES OF EQUIPMENT POSSESSED BY UNIT MUST BE RECORDED ABOVE IF IT HAS A MEQPT ID CODE KEEP ALL LIKE ITEMS TOGETHER AND ADD UP UNIT TOTALS IN MEPSA AND MEORC COLUMNS ONCE TO AID IN ENTRY. ADD UNIT TOTALS PER MEQPT ITEM ON ONLY ONE LINE ENTRY

PRINCIPLE END ITEMS (PEI):

T/E AUTHORIZED:_____

(LM2-MEE= PEI)

POSSESSED:

_____ _____ _____

DEADLINED:

_____ _____ _____

PEI SHORTAGES				PEI DEADLINED			
TAMCN	T/E AUTH	ON-HAND		TAMCN	T/E AUTH	ON-HAND	DEADLINE

NOTE: LIST THREE PEI SHORTAGES AND/OR DEADLINES WHICH CAUSE GREATEST DEGRADATION TO UNIT READINESS

C-RATINGS: S-_____ R-_____(SORTS Generated) IF C-LEVEL ENTERED, SHEET IS CLASSIFIED!

EQUIP
ON-HAND (ESRAT): MEE_____% PEI___% CONDITION (ERRAT): MEE_____% PEI_____%

NOTE: MANDATORY REASON CODE IF UNIT IS NOT C-1.

		RSN CODE	DESCRIPTION
"S"	ESRES		
"R"	ERRES		

ESRAT: MAKE A REMARK REGARDING ADDED OR GIVEN MEQPT TO ANOTHER SORTS UNIT

EXAMPLE: MEQPT ADJ, INCREASED 2 AAVC7 FROM 1/23

MANDATORY/REGULAR REMARK: ESRES - PROVIDE DETAILS ON REASON (S) FOR DEGRADATION.

"CRITICAL PEI EQUIPMENT SHORTAGES READ TAM/TE/OH:" (DO NOT USE THE REASON CODE DESCRIPTIONS) EXCESSES ARE NOTED IN REMARKS BY TYPE AND NUMBER

_____
_____
_____

MANDATORY/REGULAR REMARK: ERRES - PROVIDE DETAILS ON REASON (S) FOR DEGRADATION.

"CRITICAL PEI EQUIPMENT DEADLINES READ TAM/OH/DL:" (DO NOT USE THE REASON CODE DESCRIPTIONS)

_____
_____
_____

_____ _____
G-4/MMO SIGNATURE DATE

4. <u>CBRN Defense Worksheet</u>. Using the CBRN Readiness Calculator will greatly reduce the time required to determine the overall S-rating, eliminates the need to perform manual calculations, and provides the same results as the CBRN Equipment Worksheet. It is available for use at <u>https://ips.usmc.mil/sites/mcsccbrn/default.aspx</u>. If the Calculator will not be used, unit CBRN personnel will use the worksheet in Figure F-3 to calculate the CBRN Defense equipment rating. Apply criteria from tables 6-1 to assign the rating, and use codes from Appendix G to provide justification and amplifying remarks as required.

Figure F-3.—-CBRN Equipment Worksheet

CBRN Equipment Rating:	Calculated		Subjective	
CBRN Sense				
TAMCN and Nomenclature	Authorized	Serviceable On Hand	Percent On Hand	Rating
Chemical Detection Equipment				
C21012E Kit, Detector, Chemical Agent M256A1				
C21042E Detector, Chem Agent, Joint (JCAD) M4				
C21102E Detector, Chem Agent, Paper M9				
C23752E Kit, Testing, Water, Agents, Chem M272				
Chemical Detection Rating:				
Biological Detection Equipment				
The Marine Corps has not fielded any Biological Detection Equipment				
Biological Detection Rating:				
Radiological/Nuclear Detection Equipment	Numerical Entry Required			
A00267G Radiation Detection System AN/PDR-77				
A00817G RADIAC Set AN/UDR-13				
Radiological/Nuclear Detection Rating:				
CBRN Detection Equipment				
C21207B MAGTF CBRN Set				
CBRN Detection Equipment Rating:				
Overall CBRN Sense Rating:			Subjective Rating:	
CBRN Shield				
TAMCN and Nomenclature	Authorized	Serviceable On Hand	Percent On Hand	Rating
Ground Equipment	Numerical Entry Required			
C00432F M53 Joint Service General Purpose Mask SOF Variant				
C00512B Joint Combat Vehicle Crewman Coverall (JC3)				
C00622F Coat, UC, Overgrament, Chem Prot (JSLIST)* (Note 1)				
C00632F Trou, UC, Overgrament, Chem Prot (JSLIST)* (Note 1)				
C20102F Apron, Protective, Toxicological Agents				
C21302F Alternate Footwear Solutions*				
C21502F Glove, Protective, Chem*				
C52652E Joint Service General Purpose Mask, Field M50*				
C52662E M51 Mask, Chem-Bio (CB), Protective, CV M51				
C52692E M46 Tester, Mask Leakage, JT SVC (JSMLT) M46				
M61 Filter/Canister* (Note 2)				
M50 Canteen Cap (Note 2)				
Overall CBRN Shield Rating:			Subjective S- Rating:	

CBRN Sustain

TAMCN and Nomenclature	Authorized	Serviceable On Hand	Percent On Hand	Rating
Sustain Equipment				
B12917B Decontamination System, LTWT (M17MCHFS)				
C20752E Decontamination Kit, Skin, M291*				
C20832E Decontamination System, Sorbent (SDS) M100				
C2202E Joint Service Personnel/Skin Decon System JSPDS/RSDL*				
Overall CBRN Sustain Rating:		**Subjective Rating:**		

CBRN Medical

TAMCN and Nomenclature	Authorized	Serviceable On Hand	Percent On Hand	Rating
Medical Equipment				
C80008 Joint Biological Agent Identification and Diagnosis System				
C86878 AMAL 687, NBC Medications Per Individual				
C86888 AMAL 688, NBC Medications Per 1000 (Unit)				
Overall CBRN Medical Rating:		**Subjective Rating:**		

Note 1. All Joint Service Lightweight Integrated suit Technology coats and trousers are being replaced by the Universal Camouflage pattern. Therefore, only the TAMCNs for the Universal Camouflage pattern are included in the calculator. Units will enter the totals for the two old pattern AAOs in the appropriate Universal Camouflage pattern Authorized cell. The Serviceable On Hand is the total coats/trousers regardless of the camouflage pattern.

Note 2. Refer to the appropriate resource area below to determine the AAO/Authorized quantity for this item.

Appendix G

Readiness Tables

Table G-1.--Reason Codes

PERSONNEL	
CODE	DEFINITION
P01	Casualties
P03	MOS Imbalances
P04	Not MOS Qualified
P06	Organization Decommissioning/Deactivating
P07	Organization In Rotational Deployment
P08	Organization Recently Activated/Reorganized
P09	Personnel Deployed
P11	Personnel Shortage
P13	Personnel Shortage-Armor MOS
P14	Personnel Shortage-Artillery MOS
P15	Personnel Shortage-Combat Crews
P16	Personnel Shortage-Crew Chief
P18	Personnel Shortage-Engineer MOS
P19	Personnel Shortage-Enlisted
P20	Personnel Shortage-Enlisted Combat Crews
P21	Personnel Shortage-Ground Officer
P22	Personnel Shortage-Infantry MOS
P23	Personnel Shortage-Instructor
P24	Personnel Shortage-Instructor, Air Crew
P26	Personnel Shortage-Maintenance
P27	Personnel Shortage-Navigator/Observer
P28	Personnel Shortage-NCO, (E-4 To E-5)
P29	Personnel Shortage-NCO/Petty Officer E-5 To E-9
P31	Personnel Shortage-NCO, Staff NCO (E-6 To E-9)
P32	Personnel Shortage-Officer
P33	Personnel Shortage-Officer, Naval Flight
P34	Personnel Shortage--0-1 To 0-3
P35	Personnel Shortage--0-4 To 0-6
P36	Personnel Shortage-Pilot
P37	Personnel Shortage-Qualified To Perform MOS/NEC/AFSC Duties To Which Assigned
P40	Subordinate Organization Detached
P41	Personnel Shortage-Fuel Shortage
PUP	Reserved For Use In SECRN Field Only And Only When Commander's Judgement Changes C-Level
EQUIPMENT AND SUPPLIES ON HAND	
CODE	DEFINITION
S03	Aircraft In Storage
S04	Aircraft Not Fully Equipped

S06	Aircraft Operational Loss
S10	Ammunition Unserviceable/Suspended
S11	Awaiting Critical Modification
S13	Equipment In Administrative Storage
S14	Equipment Removed
S15	Missiles Inoperative
S16	Obsolete Equipment
S17	Organization Decommissioning/Deactivating
S18	Organization Recently Activated/Reorganized
S19	Radar Equipment Unavailable
S21	Subordinate Organization Detached
S22	Shortage-Ammunition
S24	Shortage-Attached Element
S25	Shortage-Communications Equipment
S28	Shortage-Engineering Equipment
S29	Shortage-General Supply Equipment
S31	Shortage-Repair Parts/Sales (Allowance List Item)
S32	Shortage-Repair Parts (Not Allowance List Item)
S33	Shortage-Repair Parts (Mount Out)
S34	Shortage-Repair Parts (OPSTK)
S35	Shortage-Secondary Repairable
S36	Shortage-Special Supply Equipment
S37	Shortage-Stock Supply
S38	Shortage-Supply (Marine Corps)
S39	Shortage-Supply (Navy)
S40	Shortage-Supporting Equipment
S41	Shortage-Test Equipment
S42	Shortage-Table Of Equipment
S43	Shortage-Vehicle(s)
S45	Shortage/Offload-Aircraft
S54	Aircraft Combat Loss
S55	Missiles Unserviceable
S56	Insufficient Fuel
SUP	Reserved For Use In SECRN Field Only And Only When Commander's Judgement Raised Overall C-Level

EQUIPMENT CONDITION	
CODE	DEFINITION
R00	Equipment Condition Degradations-Fuel Shortage
R01	Aircraft Grounded Safety Flight
R03	Aircraft, Scheduled Depot Level Maintenance (SDLM)
R07	Converison
R09	Damage-Battle/Combat
R11	Damaged/Inoperative-Aircraft
R12	Damaged/Inoperative-Aircraft Arresting Gear
R13	Damaged/Inoperative-Aircraft Catapults
R18	Damaged/Inoperative-ECM
R21	Damaged/Inoperative-Equipment

R22	Damaged/Inoperative-Equipment, Communications
R23	Damaged/Inoperative-Equipment, Electric Power Generating
R24	Damaged/Inoperative-Equipment, Engineering
R25	Damaged/Inoperative-Equipment,Fire Control
R28	Damaged/Inoperative-Launcher, Missile
R31	Damaged/Inoperative-Radar
R32	Damaged/Inoperative-Radar, Fire Control
R33	Damaged/Inoperative-Radar, Search
R35	Damaged/Inoperative-System, Data
R39	Damaged/Inoperative-System, Missile Fire Control
R40	Damaged/Inoperative-System, Navigation
R45	Damaged/Inoperative-Vehicle(s)
R46	Damaged/Inoperative-Weapons(s)
R51	Equipment, Obsolete
R54	Equipment Shortage
R59	Installing Field Changes/Alterations/Modifications
R61	Maintenance-In Progress, Extensive Field
R62	Maintenance-Scheduled
R63	Maintenance-Unscheduled
R64	Modification-Aircraft
R65	Not Mission Capable Maintenance (NMCM)--Aircraft Communications
R66	Not Mission Capable Maintenance (NMCM)--Aircraft Navigational
R67	Not Mission Capable Maintenance (NMCM)--Aircraft Instruments
R68	Not Mission Capable Maintenance (NMCM)--Aircraft Navigational System
R69	Not Mission Capable Maintenance (NMCS)--Aircraft Utilities
R70	Not Mission Capable Supply (NMCS)-- Aircraft Weapons Control
R71	Not Mission Capable Supply (NMCS)-- Above Organizational Maintenance
R72	Not Mission Capable Supply (NMCS)-- Aircraft Airframe
R73	Not Mission Capable Supply (NMCS)-- Aircraft
R74	Not Mission Capable Supply (NMCS)-- Aircraft Communications
R75	Not Mission Capable Supply (NMCS)-- Aircraft Instruments
R76	Not Mission Capable Supply (NMCS)-- Aircraft Navigational System
R77	Not Mission Capable Supply (NMCS)-- Aircraft Utilites
R78	Not Mission Capable Suppply (NMCS)-- Aircraft Weapons Control
R79	Not Mission Capable Supply (NMCS)-- Organizational Maintenance
R80	Organization Decommissioning/Deactivating
R81	Organization In Rotational Deployment
R82	Overhaul-Aircraft
R84	Overhaul-Weapons
R87	Repair-Attached Organizations's Equipment
R89	Repair-Electric
R90	Repair Equipment
R91	Repair-Field Maintenance
R92	Repair-Lack Proper Tools To Perform
R93	Repair-Organizational Maintenance
R94	Repair-Weapons

R95	CBRN Equipment Incomplete Or Obsolete
R97	Modification-Missile
R98	Not Mission Capable Supply (NMCS)-- Missile
R99	Overhaul-Missile
RUP	Reserved For Use In SECRN Field Only And Only When Commanders's Judgement Raised Overhall C-Level

TRAINING	
CODE	**DEFINITION**
T01	
T02	Administrative Deadline Equipment
	Deadline Rate Of Major Communications/Electronic Items
T03	Restricts Training
T04	Inadequate-Onboard Training Devices
T05	Inadequate-Range Services
T07	Inadequate-School Quotas
T08	Inadequate-Training Ammunition
T09	Inadequate-Training Areas
T10	Incomplete-Exercise/Inspections
T11	Incomplete-Firing/Proficiency Tests
T12	Insufficient-Crews Not Category 1
T13	Insufficient-Crews Not Category 1, Enlisted
T14	Insufficient-Flight Operations Marine Air Control Squadrons (MACS)
T15	Insufficient-Flight Operations Marine Air Traffic Control Unit (MATCU)
T16	Insufficient-Funding
T17	Insufficient-Naval Flights Officers Not Category 1
T21	Insufficient-Pilots Not Category 1
T22	MOS Imbalances
T23	Naval Aviation Training Operations (NATOPS) Qualifications
T24	Operational Commitments
T25	Organization Activating
T26	Organization Decommissioning/Deactivating
T28	Organization In Rotational Deployment
T29	Personnel Turnover Excessive
T30	Shortage-Amphibious Shipping
T31	Shortage-Crew Chief
T32	Shortage-Equipment
T33	Shortage-Instructor
T35	Shortage-Instructor, Pilot/Aircrew
T36	Shortage-NCO, Senior
T37	Shortage-Officer, Qualified
T38	Shortage-Personnel
T39	Shortage-Technical Skill Personnel
T40	Squad/Crew Qualification Low
T41	Tests-Unsatisfactory C-Level
T42	Training Incomplete
T43	Training Incomplete-Air Warfare (ARW)

T44	Training Incomplete-Antiair Warfare (AAW)
T52	Training Incomplete-Special Warfare (SPW)
T55	Training Incomplete-Subordinate Organization(s) Standyby Status
T56	Training Incomplete-Teams
T57	Training Incomplete-Fuel Shortage
T58	Personnel Shortage-Combat Crews
T59	Personnel Shortage-Crew Chief
T64	Casualties
T68	Insufficient-Flights Hours
TUP	Reserved For Use In SECRN Field Only And Only When Commander's Judgement Raised Overall C-Level

CBRN - TRAINING CODES	
CODE	**DEFINITION**
TNA	Insufficient Individual Protective/Survival Measures Training
TNB	Insufficient Unit Mission Oriented Task Training
TNC	Insufficient CBRN Team Training
TND	Insufficient CBRN Officer/Specialist Training
TNE	Insufficient MOPP Conditioning Training
TNF	Insufficient Personnel Completing The Mask Confidence Exercise
TNG	SHORTAGE OF TRAINED DEVICES/ASSETS
TNH	SHORTAGE OF TRAINED NBC TEAM MEMBERS
TNI	PERSONNEL SHORTAGE - NBC DEFENSE OFFICER
TNJ	PERSONNEL SHORTAGE - NBC DEFENSE SPECIALIST
TNK	NON-MISSION CAPABLE DURING RECENT NBC MCCRES/ORE/EVALUATION
TNL	ENVIRONMENTAL RESTRICTIONS ON TRAINING
TNN	HIGH TEMPERATURE TRAINING RESTRICTIONS
TNO	INADEQUATE TRAINING AMMUNITION - CS CAPSULES/GRENADES
TNP	INADEQUATE SCHOOL QUOTAS
TNQ	NEW EQUIPMENT - TRAINING NOT RECEIVED
All acronyms are identified in CJCSM 3150.02	

Table G-2.--Current Status And Activity Codes

ADMINISTRATIVE CATEGORY	
CODE	DEFINITION
AC	In Process Of Activating/Rebuilding From CADRE
DE	In Process Of Deactivating/Reducing to CADRE
ER	En Route
NP	Active ORG In CADRE Status
RD	In Process Or Reactivating
UM	Organization Not Manned Or Equipped, But Required In The Wartime Structure
XX	Organization Noneffective/NO Assets (Resulting From Hostile Action)
OPERATIONAL	
CODE	DEFINITION
CA	Actual Combat
CD	Civil Disturbance
CJ	Contingency/Joint Operation (Short Of Actual Combat/Combat Support)
CM	Organization Performing Classified Mission
CS	Combat Support
DA	Deployment Alert/Redeployment Alert
DR	Disaster Relief
OP	Organization Performing Normal Operational Mission (Short Of Actual Combat)* (note: Use Only When A More Specific Code Is Not Available)
RF	Ready/Alert Force (Alert Contingency MAGTF, Ready MEU, Alert CBIRF, etc.)
MAINTENANCE	
CODE	DEFINITION
CV	Organization Major Equipment
TRAINING	
CODE	DEFINITION
NA	RESERVE COMPONENT ORGANIZATION TRAINING OTHER THAN ANNUAL ACTIVE DUTY FOR TRAINING
TB	ANNUAL ACTIVE DUTY FOR TRAINING FOR RESERVE COMPONENT ORGANIZATION
TR	UNDERGOING TRAINING
TU	ORGANIZATION WITH THE ASSIGNED MISSION OF TRAINING OTHER ORGANIZATIONS/INDIVIDUALS
TW	ORGANIZATIONS WITH PRIMARY TASKING AS TRAINING UNIT THAT COULD BE TASKED TO PERFORM A WARTIME MISSION

TRAINING	
CODE	DEFINITION
NA	Reserve Componet Organization Training Other Than Annual Active Duty For Training
TB	Annual Active Duty For Training For Reserve Component Organization

Table G-3.-—Type Personnel Code Descriptions

CODE	DEFINITION
AC	USA Commissioned Office
AE	USA Enlisted
CP	CIV Personnel
CQ	CIV EMP (Non-US Citizen)
CS	CIV EMP (US Citizen)
EC	USCG Commissioned Officer
EE	USCG Enlisted
FC	USAF Commissioned Officer
FE	UASF Enlisted
MC	USMC Commissioned Officer/Warrant Officer
ME	USMC Enlisted
NC	USN Commissioned Officer
NE	USN Enlisted
NM	USN Midshipmen
ZA	Foreign Officers
ZC	Foreign CIV Personnel
ZE	Foreign Enlisted

Table G-4.--Deployable Personnel

Deployable Personnel
On duty in a billet that serves the overall mission of the command; to include personnel attending local command schools
Temporary Additional Duty (TAD)
Fleet Assistance Program (FAP)
Terminal leave voluntary request to transfer FMCR (not at Service limit)
Annual leave
Deferred hostile fire
Restricted as result of nonjudicial punishment
Assigned, but not departed for next duty station (PCS)
Insufficient security clearance
Exceptional family member
Request retirement
Retirement approved (voluntary request, not at Service limits)
Request transfer to FMCR
Transfer to FMCR approved (voluntary request, not at Service limits)
Request resignation
Resignation Approved

Table G-5.--Nondeployable Personnel

Nondeployable Personnel
Medical
HIV positive
Undergoing level III alcohol treatment
Sick in hospital
Not physically qualified (medical, dental, panorex)
Pregnancy (after determination by proper authority)
Postpartum (up to six months after delivery)
Dental Class 3 or 4
Physical Evaluation Board determination
Administrative
End of active service (EAS) within 7 days
Home awaiting orders (PEB)
Mandatory retirement
Terminal leave--mandatory retirement
Home awaiting administrative discharge other than for expiration of enlistment or fulfillment of service obligation
Unauthorized absence
Absentee or deserter
Captured or prisoner of war
Missing in action
Sole surviving son or daughter
Hazardous area restrictions
Legal
Confined awaiting trial by general court martial
Confined serving sentence of trial by general court martial
Confined awaiting action by higher authority
Involuntary hold beyond EAS as a special or summary court martial prisoner
On leave awaiting results of apellate review
In the hands of civilian authorities

Commander's Call
Confined awaiting trail by summary courtmartial
Confined serving sentence by summary court martial
Confined awaiting trail by special court martial
Confined serving sentence by special court martial
In the hands of military authorities
Sick in quarters
Sick in dispensary
Under investigation by military or civilian authorities
Administrative/legal hold
Light duty (1-30 days)
Physical remedial program
Temporary limited duty
Probation
Other
Undergoing primary MOS training/school
Humanitarian transfer
Humanitarian temporary additional duty
Hardship discharge approved
IA, JMD
Assigned as Individual Augmentee external to MAGTF
Assigned as Joint Military Duty external to MAGTF

Table G-6.---Percentage Employed/Deployed

CODE	PERCENT	DEFINITION
D	5-15	Percentage of Personnel Unmavailable Due to Detachments Assigned to Other Unit(s) (e.g. MEU)
E	16-25	
F	26-35	
G	36-75	

Table G-7.—Major Commands/Reporting Organizations

SERVICE	UIC	DEFINITION CODES
JOINT	DJJ010	Joint Staff
USN	N00011	Chief Of Naval Operation
	N00060	Commander, U.S. Fleet Forces Command
	N00061	Commander, U.S. Naval Forces, Europe
	N00070	Commander, U.S. Pacific Fleet
USMC	M54000	Headquarters, U.S. Marine Corps (HQMC)
	M19000	I Marine Expeditionary Force (1 MEF)
	M20000	Marine Forces Command (MARFORCOM)
	M20002	Marine Forces Southern Command (MARFORSOUTHCOM)
	M20015	Marine Forces Reserve (MARFORRES)
	M20020	Marine Forces Pacific (MARFORPAC)
	M20050	Marine Forces Northern Command (MARFORNORTHCOM)
	M20400	Marine Forces Africa Command (MARFORAFRICOM)
	M20500	Marine Forces Central Command (MARFORCENTCOM)
	M20600	Marine Forces European Command (MARFOREUCOM)
	M20700	Marine Forces Strategic Command (MARFORSTRATCOM)
	M20800	Marine Forces Korea (MARFORKOREA)
	M20900	Marine Forces Special Operations Command (MARFORSOC)
	M20120	III Marine Expeditionary Force (III MEF)
	M20130	II Marine Expeditionary Force (II MEF)
	M30600	Marine Forces Cyberspace Command (MARFORCYBERCOM)

Appendix H

Abbreviations

AAO	approved acquisition objective
ACE	aviation combat element
ACGEO	extended active duty location
ACITY	extended active duty activity
ACTIV	current status and activity code
ADATE	extended active duty date
ADCON	administrative control
ADS	authoritative data source
AMAL	authorized medical allowance list
ANAME	abbreviated organization name field
ANMCC	alternate national military command center
ARRDT	destination arrival date
AUTODIN	automatic digital network
BIDE	basic identity data element
C-level	category level
CADAT	forecasted date of change
CARAT	forecasted category level change
CARF	combat active replacement factor
CATLIMIT	category level limitation
CAX	combined arms exercise
CBD	chemical and biological defense
CBDRT	chemical biological defense readiness training
CBRN	chemical biological radiological, and nuclear
CBIRF	chemical biological incident response force
CBTCDR	combatant commander
CD&I	combat development & integration
CE	command element
CG	commanding general
CINC	commander in chief
CMC	commandant of the marine corps
CO	commanding officer
COAFF	country or international affiliation field
COCOM	combatant commander
COMMARFOR	commander marine forces
CONPLAN	concept plan
CREAL	primary duty crew allocated
CREWA	primary duty crews authorized
CREWF	primary duty crews -- formed
CRMRC	primary duty crews mission-ready -- conventional
CRMRD	primary duty crews mission-ready -- dual

CRMRN	primary duty crews mission-ready --nuclear
CRMRO	primary duty crews mission-ready -- other
CRO	command reporting organization
CS	combat support
CSE	combat support equipment
CSERV	combatant command or Service command
CSP	combat support equipment
CSS	combat service support
CSSE	combat service support element
C2	command and control
C4I	command, control, communications, computers and intelligence

DECL	downgrade and declassification
DEPS	deployable strength
DETA	estimated time of arrival at destination
DEFCON	defense readiness condition
DEPDT	origin departure date
DEPLOY	deployment status
DFCON	defense condition
DIO	drrs integration office
DISA	defense information systems agency
DL	distance learning
DMDC	defense manpower data center
DRRS	defense readiness reporting system
DTG	date-time group
DOD	department of defense

EAD	extended active duty
EDL	equipment density list
EMBRK	organization embarked
EQCONDN	equipment condition rating
EQSUPPLY	equipment and supplies-on-hand rating (set)
EDL	equipment density list
ERRAT	measured resource area rating for equipment condition
ERRES	primary reason r-rating not r-1
ESORTS	enhanced status of resources and training system
ESRAT	equipment and supplies-on-hand
ESRES	primary reason S-rating not S-1
EXER	exercise identifier

FAP	fleet assistance program
FLAG	organic unit established
FORDV	equipment foreign origin
FORECAST	forecasted category level

FTP	file transfer protocol
GAINING	gaining command
GCE	ground combat element
GELOC	geo-location code
GCCS-J	global command and control system - joint
GCCS-M	global command and control system -- maritime
GCC RWG	global command and control readiness working group
GCMD	gaining command
GEOFILE	geo-location code file
GEOLOC	geographic location code
GENTEXT	general text
GMT	greenwich mean time
GSORTS	global status of resources and training system
HQMC	headquarters, u.s. marine corps
IA	individual augmentee
IAW	in accordance with
IIF	individual issue facility
IFF	identification, friend or foe
IMA	individual mobilization augmentee
IMRL	individual material readiness list
INTR	interested command
JCS	joint chiefs of staff
JMD	joint manning document
JOPES	joint operation planning and execution system
JTF	joint task force
LABEL	data element label
LIM	category level limitation
LNAME	organization long name
LOSING	losing organization set
MAGTF	marine air-ground task force
MAJOR	major unit indicator field
MALS	marine aviation logistics squadron
MARDIV	marine division
MARES	marine corps automated readiness evaluation system
MARFOR	marine forces
MARFORCOM	marine forces command
MARFORRES	marine forces reserve
MAW	marine aircraft wing
MCTFS	marine corps total force structure system
MET	mission essential task

METL	mission essential task list
MOBCOM	mobilization command
MC	marine commissioned
MCTL	marine corps task list
MCGERR	marine corps ground equipment resource reporting system
MCO	marine corps order
MCREM-R	marine corps readiness equipment module-reserves
MCTIMS	marine corps training information management system
MDATE	scheduled mobilization day
ME	marine enlisted
MEB	marine expeditionary brigade
MEE	mission essential equipment
MEF	marine expeditionary force
MEL	mission equipment list
MENAM	major equipment name
MEORC	major equipment operationally ready - conventional
MEORD	major equipment operationally ready -- dual
MEORO	major equipment operationally ready -- other
MEPSA	major equipment authorized
MEPSD	major equipment possessed
MEQLOCN	major equipment and crew status
MEQPT	major equipment identification
MEREC	major equipment - - reconnaissance capability
MEREP	major equipment identification report
METs	mission essential task(s)
METL	mission essential task list
METAL	major equipment allocated
MEU	marine expeditionary unit
MEU(SOC)	marine expeditionary unit (special operations capable)
MJCOM	major command code
MMO	maintenance management officer
MODFG	modified location flag
MODLOC	modified location
MOS	military occupational specialty
MSC	major subordinate command
MSGID	message identifier
MTT	mobile training team
MWSG	marine wing support group
MEPSD	mee possessed
N/A	not applicable
NC	navy commissioned

NCA	national command authority
NCO	noncommissioned officer
NE	navy enlisted
NEWLOC	new location
NEWTREAD	new type report
NMCC	national military command center
NMCM	not mission capable maintenance
NORAD	north american aerospace defense command
OPCON	operational control
OPER	operation identifier
OPLAN	operation plan
OPTAR	operating target
ORGLOCN	organization and location
OSD	office of the secretary of defense
OVERALL	overall c-level
OVRRD	override sequence number
P-rating	personnel rating
PCS	permanent change of station
PCTEF	percent effective
PEI	principal end items
PEGEO	personnel geographic location code
PERSONEL	personnel level (set)
PERSTREN	personnel strength
PICDA	date of change of personnel information
PLA	plain language address
PLETD	estimated time of departure from present location
PM	program manager
PMA	primary mission area
PMAA	primary mission aircraft authorization
POINT	geographic coordinates
POSTR	possessed strength
PRRAT	measured area level for personnel
PRRES	primary reason p-level not p-1
PRGEO	present location code
PUIC	parent organization's unit identifier
R-rating	equipment condition rating
RAS-IT	readiness assessment system input tool
RAS-OT	readiness assessment system output tool
RAT	rollup across tamcns
RDATE	release date from extended active duty
READY	current overall category level
REASN	primary reason unit is not c-1
RECON	reconnaissance

RBE	remain behind element
REVAL	registration validity field
RICDA	date of change of category information
RLIM	reason for category level limitation
ROH	regular overhaul
ROT	rollup on tamcn
RPTDUIC	reported unit identification
RPTNORG	reporting organization
RPTOR	reporting organization field in rptnorg set
S-rating	equipment and supplies-on-hand rating
SAR	search and rescue
SBRPT	subordinate reporting organization
SCLAS	security classification of the entire report
SDLM	scheduled depot level maintenance
SECRN	secondary reason organization not c-1
SEQNO	sequence number of report
SHIPLOCN	ship location
SIA	site of initial activation
SIPRNET	secret internet protocol routing network
SNM	system notification message
SOCEX	special operations capable exercise
SOP	standing operating procedures
SORTS	status of resources and training system
T-rating	training rating
TAD	temporary additional duty
TA	training allowance
T/E	table of equipment
TARGT	targeted command unit identification code
TDA	table of distributions and allowances
TDATE	effective date of transfer
TDEPS	tasked deployable strength
TDY	temporary duty
TEGEO	temporary location code
TERRN	tertiary reason organization not c-1
TFSD	total force structure division
TPERS	type of personnel
TRAINING	training rating
TRANSFER	unit transfer set
TREAD	type of report
TRGEO	destination location
TRRAT	measured resource area rating for training field
TRRES	primary reason measured resource area rating for training not at c-1
T&R	training and readiness

TSOC	theater special operations command
TTs	training teams
UDC	unit descriptor code
UDP	unit deployment program
UIC	unit identification code
UIF	unit issue facility
ULC	unit level code
UNTL	universal naval task list
US	united states
USMC	united states marine corps
USMTF	united states message text format
UTC	unit type code
UTM	Unit Training Management
UTR	Unit Table of Equipment Requirement

Appendix I

Glossary

approved acquisition objective (AAO). The quantity of an item authorized for peacetime and wartime requirements to equip and sustain the Marine Corps per current DOD policies and plans.

assigned. 1. To place units or personnel in an organization where such placement is relatively permanent, and/or where such organization controls and administers the units or personnel for the primary function, or greater portion of the functions, of the unit or personnel. 2. To detail individuals to specific duties or functions where such duties or functions are primary and/or relatively permanent.

assigned mission. The mission which an organization/unit is tasked to carry out. Note: an assigned mission may also match the unit's wartime mission, i.e., purpose for which the unit was designed. Note: PCTEF is the assigned mission assessment.

assigned mission essential tasks. The METL tasks developed by the unit commander based on the mission that the unit has been directed to plan for or undertake.

assigned mission capability/readiness assessment. A commander's evaluation on their organization's ability to accomplish the mission(s) for which it was tasked.

assigned strength. The number of personnel assigned to the organization, whether they are present or not.

ad hoc unit. A unit formed to perform a particular mission in support of specific operation without consideration of wider Service application.

attachment. 1. The placement of units or personnel in an organization where such placement is relatively temporary. 2. The detailing of individuals to specific functions where such functions are secondary or relatively temporary, e.g., attached for quarters and rations; attached for flying duty.

authoritative organization (AO). An organization with oversight authority at the appropriate level for the organizing, training, and equipping of a unit. Generally, for Service units this is the Service Headquarters; for Agencies, the Office of the

Director of the Agency; for Joint units of a Combatant Command (such as Standing Joint Force Headquarters-Core Element), CCDR.

authoritative data source (ADS). A recognized or official data production with a designated mission statement or source/product to publish reliable and accurate data for subsequent use by customers. Note: an ADS may be the functional combination of multiple, separate data sources.

authorized strength. The number of billets or spaces authorized for the organization by manpower documents, a joint manning document, or by an approved DOD budget.

aviation support equipment. All equipment required to make an aeronautical system, command and control system, support system, subsystem or end item of equipment operational in its intended environment.

c-level. The C-level reflects the status of the selected unit resources measured against the resources required to undertake the wartime missions for which the unit is organized or designed. The C-level also reflects the condition of available equipment, personnel, and unit training status. C-levels, by themselves, do not project a unit's combat performance once committed to combat.

combatant command. A command with a broad continuing mission under a single commander and composed of significant assigned components of two or more Military Departments. The organization is established and so designated by the President, through the Secretary of Defense with the advice and assistance of the Chairman of the Joint Chiefs of Staff. Also called unified combatant command.

combat-essential equipment. The primary weapon system(s) or Service-designated items of gear assigned to a unit to accomplish its wartime mission.

combat leadership. Tactical leaders who provide the commander the leadership skills and qualities required to execute the unit METL and project combat power. Note: Combat Leadership assessment is applicable to the entire unit T-rating assessment and is not tied specifically to individual METs.

combat support unit. Those elements that primarily provide combat support to the combat forces and that are a part, or prepared to become a part, of a theater, command, or task force formed for combat operations.

combat service support unit. Those elements whose primary missions are to provide service support to combat forces and which are part, or prepared to become a part, of a theater, command, or task force formed for combat operations. See also operating forces; service troops; troops.

commander's assessment. A subjective evaluation by commanding officer's on the unit's ability to execute the currently assigned mission. This assessment is also known as Percent Effective (PCTEF).

composite report. A report submitted by a major unit providing an overall assessment based on condition of subordinate measured units and their ability to operate together.

core mission. Fundamental mission for which a unit was designed or organized. Core, designed, and wartime missions are the same thing.

core mission essential tasks (METs). The basic capabilities which an organization was organized or designed to perform. They draw from tasks published in MCO 3500.26_, Marine Corps Task List (MCTL), which serves as the authoritative Marine Corps publication on Marine Corps tasks.

core mission essential task list (METL). A standardized approved list of specified tasks a unit is designed or organized to perform. Selected tasks are drawn from the Marine Corps Task List (MCTL) and are standardized by type unit.

critical MOSs. Those specialties that directly affect the unit's ability to undertake its mission.

deploy. The relocation of forces, personnel, or equipment from home station to meet operational requirements.

designed mission. Fundamental mission for which a unit was designed or organized. Core, wartime, and designed missions are the same thing.

detachment. 1. A part of a unit separated from its main organization for duty elsewhere. 2. A temporary military or naval unit formed from other units or parts of units.

end-item. A final combination of end products, component parts, and/or materials that is ready for its intended use; e.g., ship, tank, mobile machine shop, aircraft.

enhanced status of resources and training system (ESORTS). Automated near real-time readiness reporting system that provides resource standards and current readiness status for operational forces and defense support organizations in terms of their ability to perform their mission essential tasks. Establishes a relationship between resource and training inputs and readiness to perform a specific MET based on standards established by the parent DOD Component. (DODD 7730.65)

equipment condition rating (R-rating). A rating which indicates the materiel condition of the organization's on-hand equipment.

equipment density list (EDL). A unit's list of combat, combat support, and combat service support equipment authorized/required for operations.

equipment and supplies on hand rating (S-rating). A rating based on a materiel measurement of an organization's on-hand posture against its designed requirement.

individual material readiness list (IMRL). A consolidated list showing items and quantities of certain aviation support equipment required for material readiness of the activity to which the list applies.

individual mobilization augmentee. An individual member of the Selected Marine Corps Reserve who receives training and is pre-assigned to fill individual military billets which augment active component structure and missions of the Marine Corps, Department of Defense and other departments or agencies of the U.S. Government to meet requirements of the organization to support mobilization requirements, contingency operations, or other specialized or technical requirements.

in-lieu of mission. A mission that is different from the designed (core/wartime) mission. An example is a tank battalion executing as a MAGTF headquarters.

in reporting status. Aircraft is in the inventory system and it requires subsystem capability impact reporting (SCIR) documentation.

installations. A grouping of facilities, located in the same vicinity, which support particular functions. Installations may be elements of a base.

intermediate level commands. They include Marine Expeditionary Forces, Marine Expeditionary Brigades (when deployed), Marine Expeditionary Units, Marine Divisions, Marine Aircraft Wings, Marine Logistics Groups, Regiments, Marine Aircraft Groups and Marine Expeditionary Force Headquarters Groups.

interface control document. A memorandum of agreement/ understanding (MOA/MOU) established between organizations that outlines intersystem-access authorizations to applications and data base information.

joint readiness. The combatant commander's or Joint Task Force Commander's ability to integrate and synchronize ready combat, and support forces to conduct assigned missions

Marine automated readiness evaluation system (MARES). It is a command information system with an overall objective to provide information concerning ground equipment status of MARFOR units and selected commands. MARES retrieves, integrates, and processes unit-provided supply and maintenance management data. It reflects the actual operational status of reportable mission-essential equipment (MEE) and principal end items (PEI), end item ground equipment possessed (on-hand) by reporting units.

Marine Corps total force structure system (MCTFS). The authoritative source for unit personnel status, and used to determine Assigned Strength. It also records, processes, and maintains personnel and pay data for all active, reserve, and retired personnel.

measured unit. Combat, combat support, and combat service support units of the operating forces, including Active, National Guard, Reserve and provisional units, apportioned to or deployed in support of an OPLAN, a CONPLAN, a SIOP, a Service war-planning document, or assigned in the 'Forces For Unified Commands' document are designated as measured units. Provisional, task-organized and "ad hoc" combat, combat support, and combat service support units of each Service, combatant command are also designated as measured units.

military occupational specialty (MOS). The grouping of duty positions requiring similar qualifications and the performanced of closely related duties.

mission. 1. The task, together with the purpose, that clearly indicates the action to be taken and the reason therefore. 2. In common usage, especially when applied to lower military units, a duty assigned to an individual or unit; a task.

mission capability assessment. The commander's assessment of his organization's ability to accomplish its mission.

mission capable aircraft. Aircraft that is/are able to perform at least one and potentially all of its missions.

mission essential equipment (MEE). MEE are items of equipment whose availability is essential and indispensable for the execution of the mission of the unit in support of a combatant commander. Items designated as MEE are of such importance that they are subject to continuous monitoring throughout the DoD Note: MEE is reportable in MARES. However, final decision for MEE lies with the Joint Staff.

mission essential task. An activity (task) selected by a commander, deemed critical to mission accomplishment. Essential is defined as absolutely necessary; indispensible; critical.

mission essential task list (METL). The command's list of METs (tasks, conditions, and standards) considered essential for accomplishment of the unit's missions.

MOS fill. The number of personnel matched against the T/O line number billets by MOS (using the primary or secondary MOS but not both).

named operations. Named operations are those operations designated as such by the Joint Chiefs of Staff, e.g. Operation IRAQI FREEDOM. The METs for Named Operations are also known as assigned mission METLs.

non-deployable personnel. Personnel assigned to a reporting unit that are not physically present, cannot be present within the prescribed response time, or are restricted from deploying or employing with the unit. Note: non-deployable service members degrade a unit's personnel strength. Non-deployable personnel are identified by the types of personnel using non-deployable codes.

Enclosure (1)

out of reporting status. Aircraft is in the inventory reporting system, but does not require subsystem capability impact reporting documentation.

partial unit deployment. An element that deploys separately from its parent unit. It is applicable when a unit deploys only a part or portion of its mission capability to support an operation. It applies to small unit elements that are not registered in GSORTS separately from their parent unit.

percent effective (PCTEF). The current percent of effectiveness of the organization. Commander's subjective assessment of the unit's ability to execute its currently assigned mission. Note: It is referred to as the assigned mission assessment in DRRS-MC.

personnel available. Personnel are considered available if they are assigned to a reporting unit, are physically present or can be present within the prescribed response time, and are not restricted from deploying or employing with the unit for any reason.

personnel rating (P-Rating). A personnel resource rating determined by the lowest percentage between personnel strength and MOS fill.

possessed/on-hand strength. Total number of military personnel physically present with an organization (including personnel present for temporary duty).

principal end items (PEIs). Ground equipment that has been nominated by either DC I&L, MARFORS or supporting commands i.e. LOGCOM, SYSCOM as reportable in the Marine Corps Automated Readiness Evaluation System (MARES). PEIs are equipment whose serviceability/operational capability do not undergo frequent inspection or can not be readily replaced by the unit's first source of supply. PEI's have been designated as combat essential in the Total Force Structure Management Information System (TFSMIS), and are of sufficient range to provide an adequate measure of overall equipment status or capability for MARFORs.

provisional unit. A Service or combatant commander directed temporary assembly of personnel and equipment organized for a limited period of time for accomplishment of a specific mission.

readiness. The ability of U.S. military forces to fight and meet the demands of the national military strategy. Readiness is the synthesis of two distinct but interrelated levels.

registered unit. Active, National Guard, and Reserve forces apportioned to CJCS/combatant command directed OPLANs, CONPLANs, a SIOP, Service war planning documents, or assigned in the 'Forces For Unified Commands' document. These units are created in the system database with a unique unit identification code (UIC) and a basic identity data element (BIDE) set describing the unit.

remain behind personnel (RBP)/equipment (RBE). Note: Personnel that remain behind; may or may not be in a non-deployable status. RBE may or may not impact a unit's ability to carry out its designed mission.

resource ratings. Three criteria on personnel and materiel resources (P, S, and R ratings) used by reporting units to help determine an overall readiness level.

s-rating. The equipment and supplies resource rating used by reporting units to help determine an overall readiness level.

standard depot level maintenance (SDLM). Aircraft or equipment that are enroute to, awaiting, or undergoing repair at a depot.

structured strength. The wartime manpower requirements for an organization shown on Service documents (TFSMS).

subordinate unit standards. Those criterion that reflect capabilities required by subordinate organizations in order for the higher level unit to perform specific tasks.

support equipment. One of the two major categories of equipment in GSORTS that includes, but is not limited to, equipment in unit's allowance lists, war readiness spares kits, repair parts, test equipment, and other Service-directed items of equipment for the organization to perform the mission for which organized or designed.

table of organization and equipment. A document that prescribes the wartime mission, capabilities, organizational structure, and equipment and personnel requirements for military organizations.

table of equipment requirement. Equipment required by T/E to provide designed capabilities.

tasked. Assignment to perform a specific mission or task allotted by higher component.

task organized unit. A temporary grouping of forces designed to accomplish a particular mission. Task organization involves the distribution of available assets to subordinate control headquarters by attachment or by placing assets in direct support or under the operational control of the subordinate.

task-organizing. The act of designing an operating force, support staff, or logistic package of specific size and composition to meet a unique task or mission. Characteristics to examine when task-organizing the force include, but are not limited to: training, experience, equipage, sustainability, operating environment, enemy threat, and mobility.

total force structure management system (TFSMS). Total Force Structure Management System (TFSMS) is an enterprise system that combines manpower and equipment data for the purpose of managing the Total Force. The primary mission of TFSMS is to serve as the primary data source and business process engine for the activities defined in Marine Corps Order 5311.1D.

training allowance. A reduced portion of a Reserve unit's AAO [UTR] needed to conduct home station training.

training rating (T-rating). A rating based on the percentage of METs trained to standard.

unit descriptor code. A code indicating the component general status and primary mission for which the organization was established.

unit identification code (UIC). A code that uniquely identifies each Active, Reserve, and National Guard unit of the Armed Forces.

unit readiness. The ability to provide capabilities required by the combatant commanders to execute their assigned missions. It is derived from the ability of each unit to deliver the outputs for which it was designed.

unit T/E requirement (UTR). Wartime requirement at the Unit Identification Code (UIC) level for a specific TAMCN. Formerly called the unit approved acquisition objective in the Total Force Structure Management System.

U.S. Armed Forces. The Army, Navy, Air Force, Marine Corps, and Coast Guard.

wartime mission. The fundamental mission for which a unit was designed or organized. Wartime, core, and designed missions are the same.

wartime resources. Personnel, equipment and organic supply assets required to accomplish a unit's wartime mission.

wartime requirements. Doctrinally established requirements needed by type units to full perform as designed and as part of the total force.